# Puppet Mania!

John E. Kennedy

**NORTH LIGHT BOOKS**

CINCINNATI, OHIO

www.artistsnetwork.com

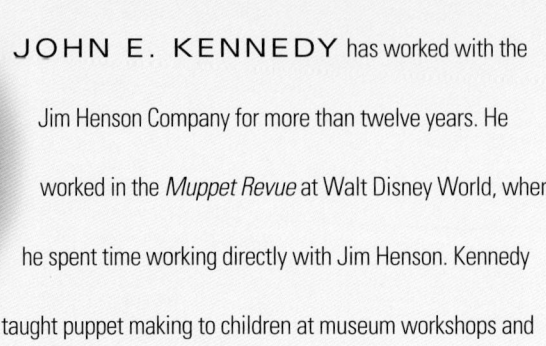

**JOHN E. KENNEDY** has worked with the Jim Henson Company for more than twelve years. He worked in the *Muppet Revue* at Walt Disney World, where he spent time working directly with Jim Henson. Kennedy has taught puppet making to children at museum workshops and has worked on *Dinosaurs, Sesame Street, The Wubbulous World of Dr. Seuss* and *Muppets from Space*. He lives in Ocoee, Florida.

**Puppet Mania!** Copyright © 2004 by Hands in Art, Inc. Printed in Singapore. All rights reserved. The patterns and drawings in the book are for the personal use of the reader. By permission of the author and publisher, they may be either hand-traced or photocopied to make single copies, but under no circumstances may they be resold or republished. It is permissible for the purchaser to make the projects contained herein and sell them at fairs, bazaars and craft shows. No other part of this book may be reproduced in any form or by any electronic or mechanical means, including information storage and retrieval systems, without permission in writing from the publisher, expect by a reviewer, who may quote a brief passage in a review. Published by North Light Books, an imprint of F&W Publications, Inc., 4700 East Galbraith Road, Cincinnati, Ohio 45236. (800) 289-0963. First edition.

08 07 06 05 04   5 4 3 2 1

Library of Congress Cataloging-in-Publication Division
Kennedy, John E.
    Puppet mania: the world's most incredible puppet making book ever / John E. Kennedy.
        p. cm.
    ISBN 1-58180-372-9
    1. Puppet making. I. Title.
TT174.7.K46 2003
745.592'24—dc21                    2003059965

Editor: David Oeters
Designer: Stephanie Strang
Layout Artist: Karla Baker
Production Coordinator: Sara Dumford
Photographers: Tim Grondin, Al Parrish and Harvey Smith
Photo Stylist: Jan Nickum

## metric conversion chart

| TO CONVERT | TO | MULTIPLY BY |
|---|---|---|
| Inches | Centimeters | 2.54 |
| Centimeters | Inches | 0.4 |
| Feet | Centimeters | 30.5 |
| Centimeters | Feet | 0.03 |
| Yards | Meters | 0.9 |
| Meters | Yards | 1.1 |
| Sq. Inches | Sq. Centimeters | 6.45 |
| Sq. Centimeters | Sq. Inches | 0.16 |
| Sq. Feet | Sq. Meters | 0.09 |
| Sq. Meters | Sq. Feet | 10.8 |
| Sq. Yards | Sq. Meters | 0.8 |
| Sq. Meters | Sq. Yards | 1.2 |
| Pounds | Kilograms | 0.45 |
| Kilograms | Pounds | 2.2 |
| Ounces | Grams | 28.4 |
| Grams | Ounces | 0.04 |

# This book is dedicated to the creative child in all of us.

The willingness to try something new diminishes as we get older and we tend to accept ourselves as we are. I hope this book can break those barriers and help people of all ages discover new ways of artistic expression.

**Acknowledgment** ☆ I want to thank my parents, Don and Doreatha Kennedy, for allowing me to keep their house constantly cluttered with foam and fur for much of my childhood and for supporting my career choice even when it didn't seem practical. ☆ My Uncle Paul and Aunt Emily, thanks for opening my eyes to art and culture outside of my Plainfield, Indiana, home. ☆ My great friend Ed Lucas and his family who helped us get a puppet business going when we were still in elementary school. ☆ Rick and Linda Baughn, thanks for letting Gary, Randy and I tear apart your living room to make puppet videos during high school summer vacation. ☆ This book wouldn't be possible without the continued enthusiasm of my business partners Mike Lanza and Max Blanchard. ☆ For his wonderful photos, I want to thank Harvey Smith, www.harveysmithphoto.com. Thanks Harvey. ☆ I want to thank my sister, Julie Kennedy-Rick, for always being there to save me on my puppet projects at the last minute. ☆ And finally, thanks to my wife, Julie M. Kennedy. You have given me the courage to share my voice.

# ✱ Table of Contents

INTRODUCTION *page 6*

TOOLS AND MATERIALS *page 8*

TECHNIQUES *page 9*

BRINGING THE PUPPET TO LIFE *page 10*

ADDRESSING THE AUDIENCE *page 12*

BODY MOVEMENTS *page 13*

## Puppet Projects *page* **16**

**1 Coaster Creature** *page 18*

**2 Bottle Bug** *page 22*

**3 Sock Puppy** *page 26*

**4 Convert-a-Bear** *page 30*

**5 Sock Turtle** *page 34*

**6 Banana Buddy** *page 38*

**7 Picture Puppet** *page 42*

**8 Running Rabbit** *page 46*

**9 Boxing Kangaroo** *page 52*

**10 Nutty Bear** *page 56*

**11 Bowl of a Thousand Faces** *page 62*

**12 Spoon Chicken** *page 68*

**13 Dancin' Chick** *page 72*

RESOURCES *page 78*

INDEX *page 79*

# *Introduction

**Puppet making has been a fantastic adventure for me, one that began when I was a child.** When I was three years old, I asked my mom if she would make a puppet for me. She let me use her bag of fabric scraps to make my own. She had no idea what she had started. I kept the house covered in felt and fur until the day I moved out.

I remember when I was twenty-two years old and leaving home for the first time to work for Walt Disney World in Florida. Every puppet I had built had been a step to getting this job, and I was proud of myself for not giving up my dream. I packed up my patterns and puppets and started my first big assignment as a professional puppeteer.

Since then I've worked on movies, TV shows and commercials, waiting for the day I might share my knowledge with others who want to make puppets. Well, this is it, the moment I've been waiting for, and I'm glad you're here to see what I've been keeping secret all these years.

Many of the puppets in this book are ones I made when I was a kid. They are easy-to-make, cool and fun. These are the puppets that people want to pick up, play with and figure out how they work. But that's not all you'll find in this book. I've collected many of my puppeteering secrets. Secrets like finding a personality for each of your puppets, dance moves and cool expressions guaranteed to get a reaction from your audience and really bring the puppets to life.

When I was younger, I used to go to the library and look up every book about puppetry I could find. I wish I could have found a book that would have shown me how to build and perform interesting and fun puppets that my audience would be as excited about as I was. This book is the answer to my dreams and my answer to everyone who has ever asked me, "How do I make a puppet?"

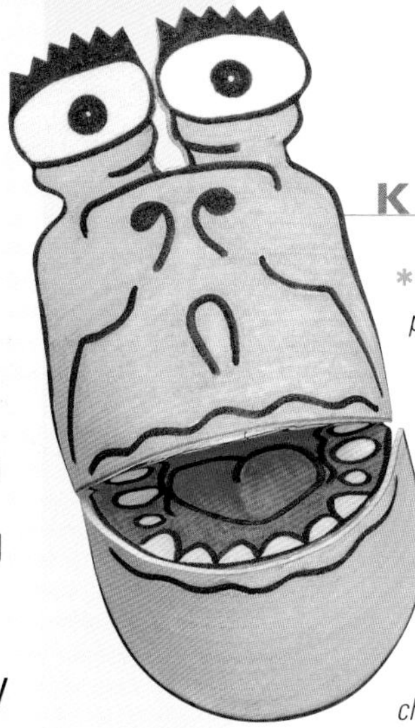

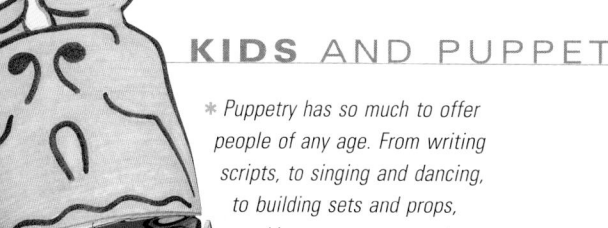

## KIDS AND PUPPETS

\* Puppetry has so much to offer people of any age. From writing scripts, to singing and dancing, to building sets and props, making your own puppet production is a great way to flex your creative muscles. It's also a wonderful social activity. Whether you're making the costumes or playing the lead character, you must have respect for all the members of the cast and crew who are working hard for the same vision. Nothing is better than the cheers of the crowd when the show is over!

I believe there are many great benefits to using puppets with kids. The creative journey a child's mind must take when making a puppet is a mental exercise that has powerful developmental rewards. Puppetry influences artistic abilities and social skills and can break mental barriers. It's a chance for kids to experiment and discover skills in themselves they didn't know they had. This can encourage a higher level of self-worth and instill a child with moral accountability for their actions.

I feel that I have been positively affected by my puppetry and invite everyone to visit me on my Web site. There you will find more information about me and my puppet career, as well as some fun activities and tips that support the material in this book. My Web address is **www.puppetkit.com**.

See you there!

# *Tools and Materials

## * PUPPET CRAFTING ESSENTIALS

BEFORE YOU BEGIN MAKING YOUR PUPPETS, you'll need to gather tools and materials. Here are my "Crafting Essentials" that every puppet maker should have on hand before starting a project. **SCISSORS:** You will need scissors for every project in this book. Because you will be cutting through some thick materials like foam and fur, you will need a good pair of sharp scissors. Always make slow, deliberate cuts, and never use a jerky motion with scissors. **GLUE:** I use a glue gun for most of the projects in the book, because hot glue sets so quickly. Craft glue and contact cement are good alternatives.

**MARKERS:** A marker is a pen that saturates paper or fabric with color. For some projects you might have to use a permanent marker to prevent bleeding when you touch the finished puppet. Acrylic paint is a good alternative. **POM-POMS:** These plush craft balls come in variety packs of different colors and sizes and are found in craft stores. Pom-poms are great for noses, eyes, teeth and paw pads and don't need any shaping; you just glue them on. Alternatives include buttons, wooden balls and plastic grapes. **FELT:** A thin, fibrous material, felt is a good all-purpose fabric that can be sewed, glued and tied into any number of projects. Felt is great for quickly adding color and external touches like puppet pockets, vests and ties. Alternatives include flannel, polar fleece and sheet foam.

**FOAM RUBBER:** Sometimes called cushion foam, foam rubber is a soft, pliable material. Its light weight and ability to be carved make it useful for puppet making. It can be found in some fabric shops, upholstery shops and packaging companies. Alternatives include batting and Styrofoam. **SHEET FOAM:** Also called craft foam, sheet foam is an extremely dense and rubbery material. Sheet foam offers many opaque colors and wears very well. It is great for making tongues, teeth and eyes. If you use a hair dryer on a warm setting to soften the foam, you can shape sheet foam to make hats, shoulder pads, shoes and armor. It can be found in craft stores. Felt is a good alternative. **FAKE FUR:** This fuzzy, furlike material with a cloth backing comes in two fur lengths: short shag fur and long shag fur. It can be found in fabric shops and craft stores. Long shag fur can be trimmed with scissors to get a real animal look. Alternatives include a feather boa, crepe hair, pipe cleaners or a wig.

# * Techniques

**HERE ARE SOME TECHNIQUES I PICKED UP** along the way that have saved me a lot of puppet-crafting time and energy. Being patient when working through the steps of a project is the key to being safe. If you take your time, you'll be more aware of what you're doing and have more control over the final look of your puppet.

## * USING A HOT GLUE GUN

A glue gun can be dangerous if you aren't careful. Move your glue gun slowly, evenly and steadily when making a line of glue. The glue can dry quickly, so glue short sections and press the material together to lock the fibers while the glue is still warm.

▶ **Make sure your hands aren't too close to the hot end of the glue gun.**

## * TRACING PATTERNS

I copy my patterns onto posterboard to keep them from buckling. Label the patterns and store them in a plastic bag. Use a permanent marker for tracing, so the pattern won't rub off on your hands. You can change the size of your project by enlarging or reducing the pattern on a copy machine or an opaque projector.

▶ **Save patterns to reuse them for more puppets.**

## * SEWING TECHNIQUES

### HOT GLUE GUN **TIPS**

\* *Always have an adult supervise a child using a glue gun!*

\* *Never leave the glue gun turned on when it's not in use. Never leave the room when a glue gun is turned on.*

\* *You can regulate the flow of the glue by pressing the tip of the glue gun against the material.*

\* *Use the glue sparingly. If you use too much glue it could ooze and damage your material or burn you.*

\* *Never leave a completed puppet that was made with hot glue in a hot car. The heat will melt the glue and you could have a ruined puppet.*

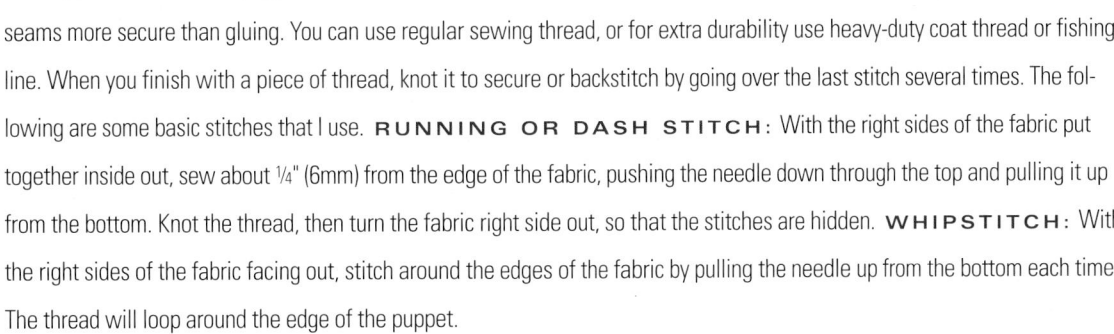

Sewing your fabric and fur puppets will make the seams more secure than gluing. You can use regular sewing thread, or for extra durability use heavy-duty coat thread or fishing line. When you finish with a piece of thread, knot it to secure or backstitch by going over the last stitch several times. The following are some basic stitches that I use. **RUNNING OR DASH STITCH:** With the right sides of the fabric put together inside out, sew about ¼" (6mm) from the edge of the fabric, pushing the needle down through the top and pulling it up from the bottom. Knot the thread, then turn the fabric right side out, so that the stitches are hidden. **WHIPSTITCH:** With the right sides of the fabric facing out, stitch around the edges of the fabric by pulling the needle up from the bottom each time. The thread will loop around the edge of the puppet.

## * FABRIC DYE TECHNIQUES

I suggest using fabric dye for some of the projects. Dyeing foam and fabric can be a great addition to a project, but take care and follow all the warnings and instructions with the dye. It can stain your hands and sink. Some good alternatives to dye include permanent markers, acrylic paints and fabric paints. Or take your project to an airbrush artist, who can add any color to foam or fabric and create highlights and shadows.

# *Bringing the Puppet to Life

## WELCOME TO A QUICK LOOK AT PUPPETEERING TECHNIQUES

and your first lessons in acting with your puppet. This is an introduction to my secret techniques for creating puppet characters.

### * FINDING INSPIRATION

Every puppet you perform with should have a unique personality. The personality of the puppet gives focus to how you will perform your puppet, its reactions and how it speaks its lines. Is your puppet happy, silly or sad? You can find puppet personality inspiration everywhere; you just need to train your eye to see the potential puppets.

- ▶ Go to a public place where you can watch people's actions and attitudes. The way someone walks or talks might be a great character idea.
- ▶ You might even already know someone who would make a good puppet. Someone you know could inspire you to make a puppet.
- ▶ As you work on the personality of your puppet, imagine asking your puppet some questions, like what is the puppet's favorite color, what hobbies does the puppet have and what kind of songs does it like? Imagine what answers the puppet might give you and write them down. They'll help bring the puppet to life, and you could even use the answers in a performance.

### * SHOWING YOUR PUPPET'S PERSONALITY

Once you have a personality for the puppet, it is time to think about the range of expressions your puppet will have, because these expressions will be your most important way of communicating the puppet's personality to the audience. The best way to get fantastic expressions from your character is to believe your puppet is real. Have the puppet react to events in the real world. It will come alive if you can show its emotions through expressions as well as dialogue. Look at how Sock Puppy uses his eye focus and mouth poses to show his emotions. Check out page 26 to make your own Sock Puppy.

## Puppeteering Secret #1

When you perform with an audience, remember the expressions you practice. Use them as a reaction to something the audience says, and your puppet will appear even more alive.

▼ **Envious** Splay your fingers wide and push your thumb to one side.

▼ **Love-Struck** Bring your thumb and pinky to the bottom corners of the mouth and push down hard with your index, middle and ring fingers.

▼ **Proud** Bring your thumb and pinky to the bottom corners of the mouth and push down slightly with your index, middle and ring fingers.

▼ **Angry** Drop your index and ring fingers below your thumb and middle finger.

▼ **Frightened** Open your fingers and thumb as wide as they'll go and tilt your wrist down.

▼ **Hurt** Tuck your thumb in and under your fingers.

▼ **Satisfied** Tuck your thumb into your palm and fingers and tilt your wrist back.

▼ **Surprised** Push your fingers and thumb forward and separate them slightly.

▼ **Confused** Twist your thumb and fingers sideways.

## ✳ FINAL THOUGHT

These poses will move your audience if you practice and perfect them. However, you can maximize the audience's response by making the expressions appear bigger than they really are. The trick is to go from one extreme expression to another. For example, move Sock Puppy slowly into a love-struck pose and then jam him into a frightened one. If you can find a theatrical reason why Sock Puppy would be head-over-heals in love and then be suddenly frightened you will get a huge reaction from your audience.

# ✱ Addressing the Audience

**BECAUSE PUPPETRY IS AN ACTION-DRIVEN CRAFT,** it is important to first experiment with what your puppet can do. The basic moves of the puppet will be the easiest to do and most often will get the best reactions from an audience.

For some puppets, lip-synching, or the way a character moves its mouth as it speaks, is the most basic move of the puppet. Lip-synching can be tricky. Opening the mouth on the vowel sounds of words and for the right amount of syllables without flapping too much is important. The only way to get better at it is to practice. You can practice by having your puppet sing along to music CDs or to the radio. I used to test my lip-synch skills to a live news report. This was hard because I didn't know what was going to be said next.

## ✱ FINAL THOUGHT

It is important that you keep practicing your lip-synch skills until they become an unconscious action. If you don't have to concentrate on the mouth movements, you free yourself to make other body movements that will make your performance even better.

## Puppeteering Secret #2

The secret to lip-synching is to make sure your puppet focuses as it speaks. To make Sock Puppy lip-synch smoothly and believably, drop your wrist, let your hand and thumb relax and push your fingers forward to the point where Sock Puppy is looking. If you don't push your fingers toward the focus point, Sock Puppy will lose his focus and it won't look like he is actually talking to the audience. It will just seem like he is flapping his mouth.

▼ **My hand closed**

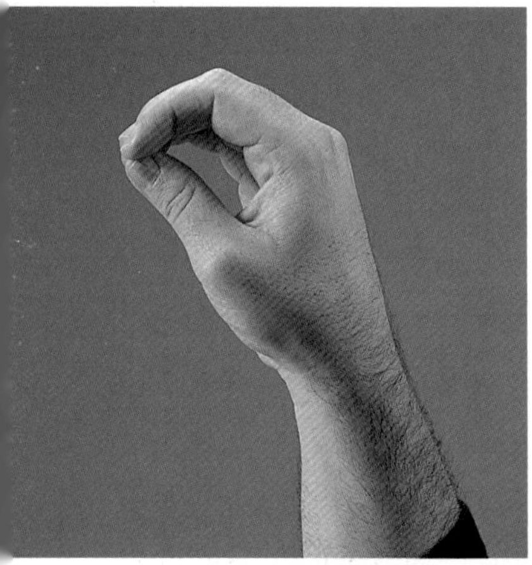

▼ **My hand open**

▼ **Sock Puppy's mouth closed**

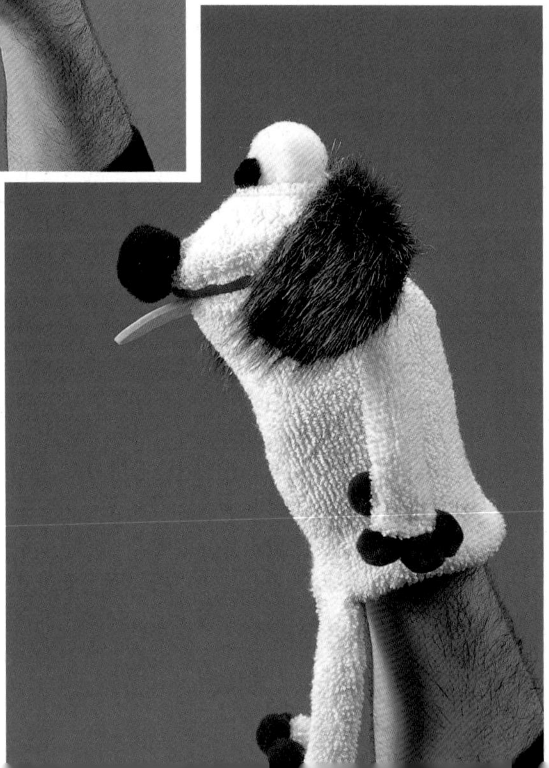

▼ **Sock Puppy's mouth open**

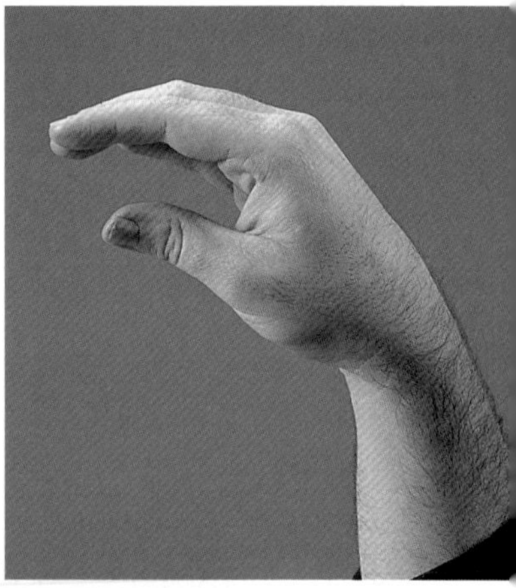

# ✳ Body Movements

TO SHOW YOU HOW TO MAKE BODY MOVEMENTS, I'd like to take you back-stage. There you can see how I place my hands to get the moves that I want. Some of the moves are specific to these puppets, but if you make a puppet with similar mechanics, these moves will apply to them, as well.

## ✳ PUPPETS WITH EYE MOVEMENT

Nutty Bear is going to help me out with this one. This puppet has an effect as its major movement. I like to show off a specialty move like eyelids by getting really good at find-ing the best poses and being able to get to them quickly. Nutty Bear can wink at the crowd or show surprise with just a quick move.

### ☆ Puppeteering Secret #3

Because his main movement is facial expres-sions Nutty Bear is a great puppet to have talk to an audience. Turn to page 56 for instruction on making your own Nutty Bear.

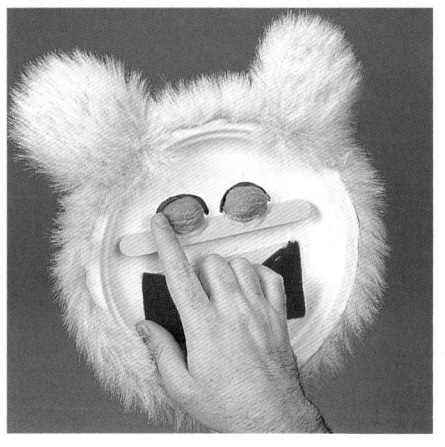
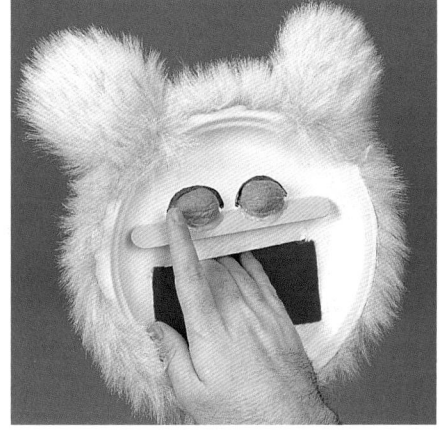
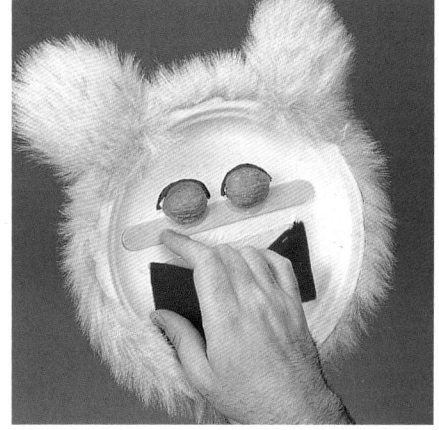

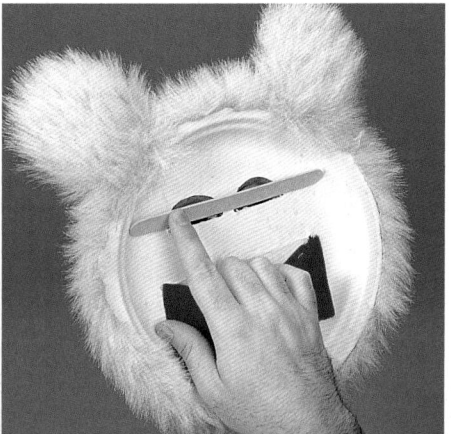

1 Listening **Put the eyes at neutral and close the mouth.** 2 Speaking **Put the eyes at neutral and open the mouth (remember to lip-synch).** 3 Surprise **Open the eyes wide and close the mouth.** 4 Sleeping **Close both the eyes and the mouth.**

# Puppeteering Secret #4

Puppets like Dancin' Chick can be tricky to use, but the audience loves them. You might need lots of practice with Dancin' Chick. Turn to page 72 to make your own Dancin' Chick.

## ✳ PUPPETS WITH BODY RODS

The Dancin' Chick is a puppet with body rods. I like to make cool poses and then find rhythmical ways to get to them that work as a dance move.

▲ **Dance Left**

**Lift the left leg.**

▲ **Dance Right**

**Lift the right leg.**

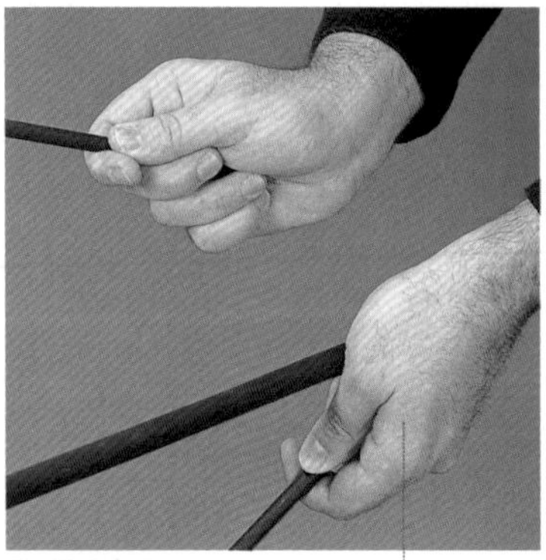

▼ **Show Dance**

**Lift the leg up and out.**

▼ **The Splits**

**Push both legs out. This is great as a big finale for a show.**

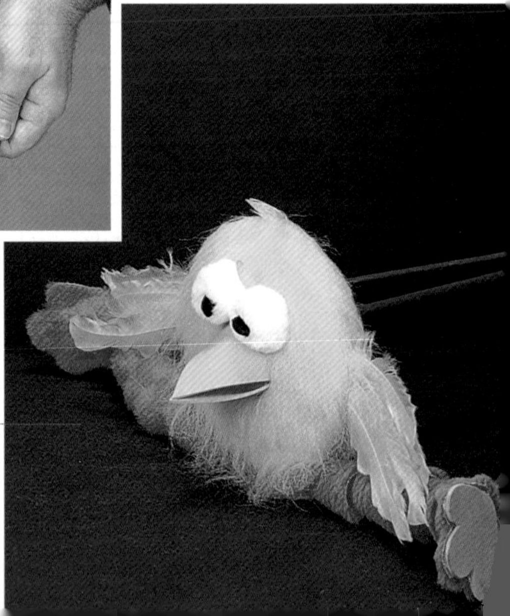

# Puppeteering Secret #5

On a puppet with arm rods, if you bend the arm wire wider at the base of the V, you will spread the gloves farther apart. Now grip the wire higher to squeeze and release. This will take the pressure off of the bend point and allow the gloves to make a lively spring to their new position. Turn to page 52 to find out how to build Boxing Kangaroo.

## ✳ PUPPETS WITH ARM RODS

I like doing big and specific moves when performing with arm rods. The way to do this is to separate the arm moves from the body moves. Don't be afraid to overact with Boxing Kangaroo.

## ✳ PUTTING IT ALL TOGETHER

The secret to using the body moves of a puppet is practicing each of the puppet's best moves, so you can use each move in a performance quickly and easily. Practice with the puppet, moving to and from each of the best moves until you can do it without any effort, even while lip-synching, using a special puppet expression or singing.

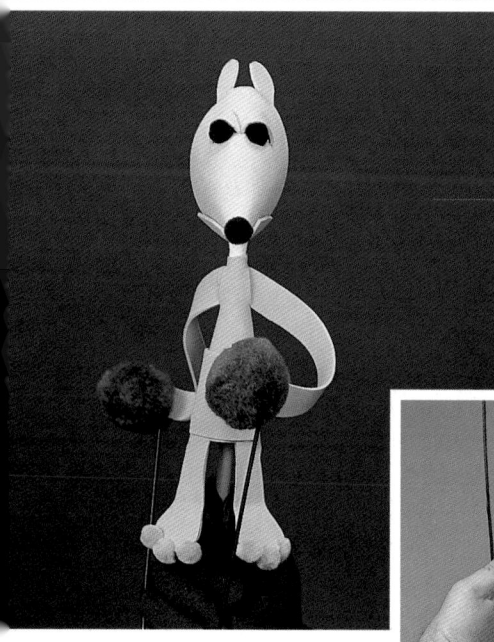

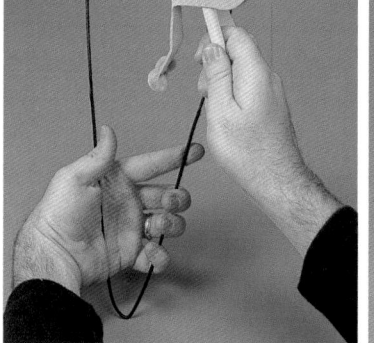

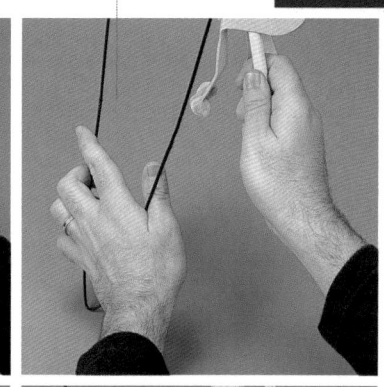

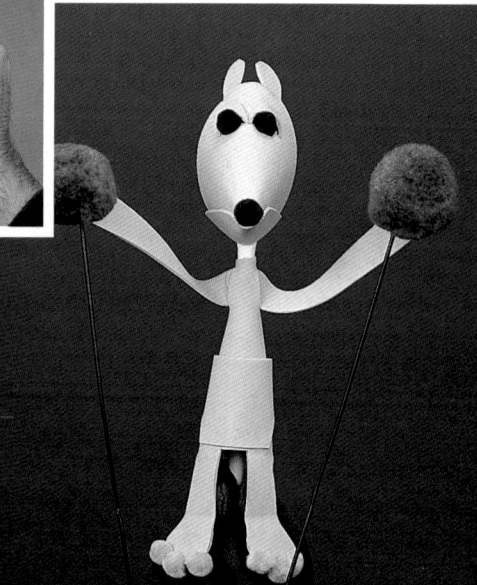

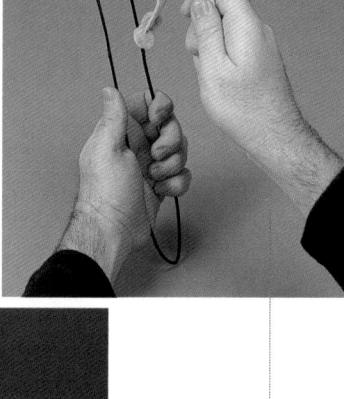

▲ **Left Punch**
**Spin the arm rod to the left.**

▼ **Boxing Handshake**
**Bring the gloves together and push forward.**

▲ **Right Punch**
**Spin the arm rod to the right.**

▼ **Victory Pose**
**Push the arm rods up.**

# *Puppet Projects

**E**very project in this book has a story to tell. The Nutty Bear puppet, for example, comes from a trip to New York City. I was eight and my parents went sightseeing one day, leaving my sister and me with my aunt. I was bored so I decided to pass the time by making a paper bag puppet. I had seen a walnut on my aunt's kitchen counter and I had a creative idea. I took the two shell halves and glued them to the tops of the eyes to make moving eyelids. They were great because I could move them with my fingers and still make the mouth talk. This was the idea I had for Nutty Bear.

As you make puppets, you'll collect stories for each one you make. You should experiment and try new things as you work on these projects! Your own creativity is the most important part of every puppet you make, so never be afraid to do something different with each project.

At the beginning of every project, you'll find a materials list. Whenever possible, I used materials that would be easy to find, stuff you might have just lying around the house, because nothing is worse than searching for materials when you want to make a puppet. I also added some ideas for alternative materials that might be easier to find or could be more appropriate for smaller puppet builders.

I've had fun piecing together the projects that came from my childhood, and now they satisfy the child that's still in me. I hope, whatever your age, they'll bring out the child in you.

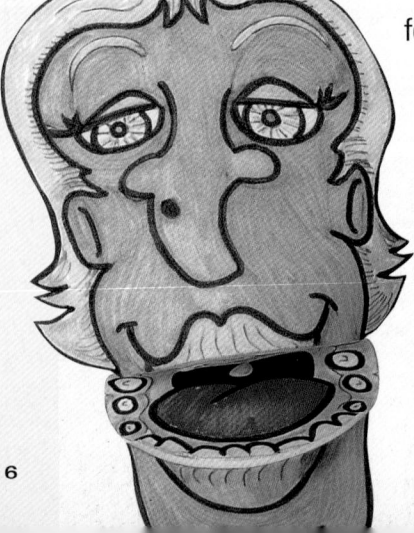

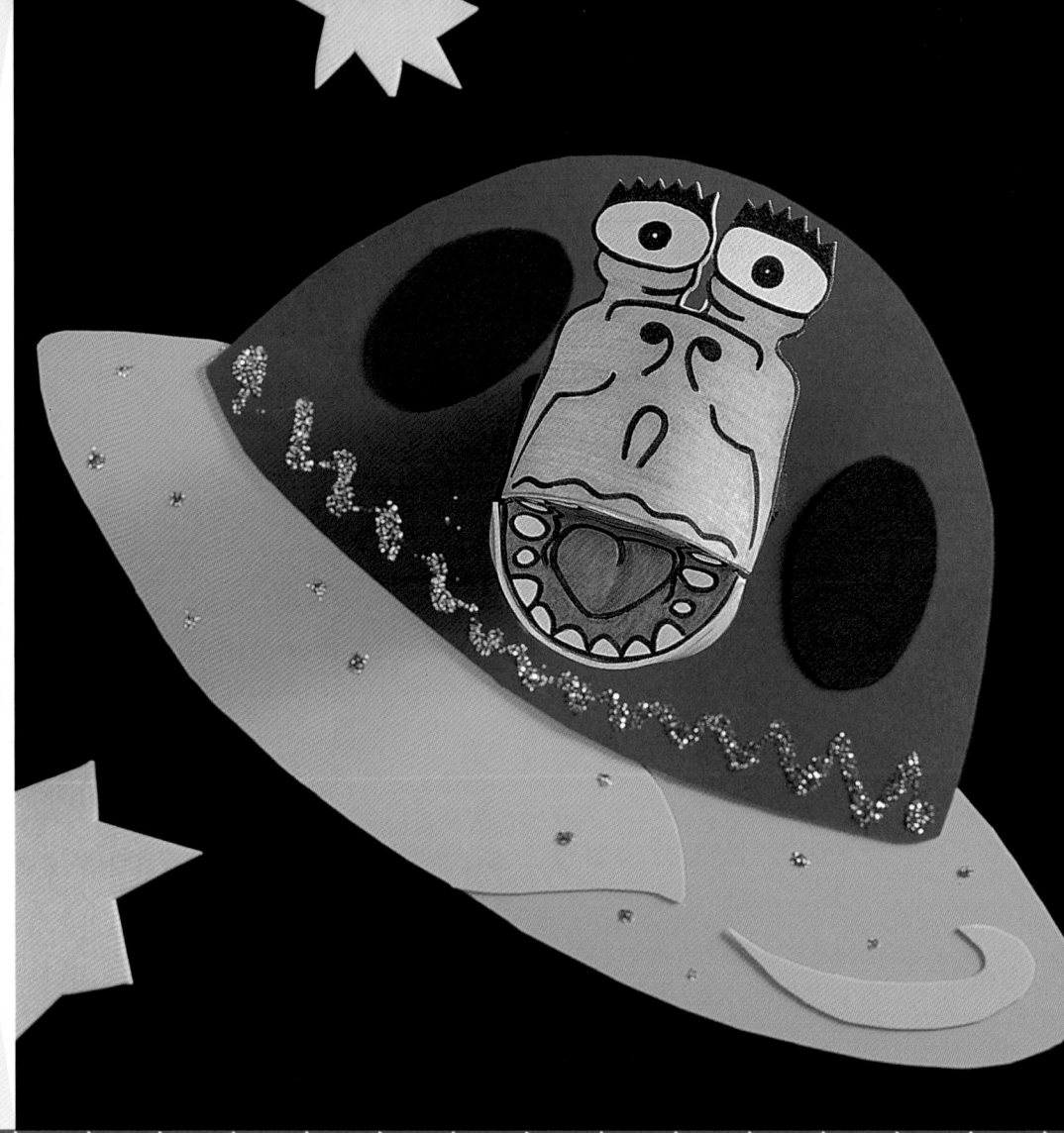

## MATERIALS

7½" x 6½" (19cm x 17cm) piece of white sheet foam

colored permanent markers or acrylic paint: green, pink and red

black permanent marker

pencil

scissors

hot glue gun or craft glue

# COASTER CREATURE

**puppet** 1 ▶ My uncle worked for a publishing company in New York for many years. Once when I was visiting him in his office, he showed me a book about masks. An idea hit me: I could make a puppet book that featured a paper puppet mouth and paper masks that could be glued to the mouth. I never wrote that book, but that idea eventually became the Coaster Creature. The Coaster Creature is a puppet face glued to a mouth.

The Coaster Creature is an easy, fun project that makes a great gift. Imagine your guests' surprise when they pick up their glasses and see a monster glaring at them! You can use the pattern to make as many creatures as you want, and each one is a useful drink coaster.

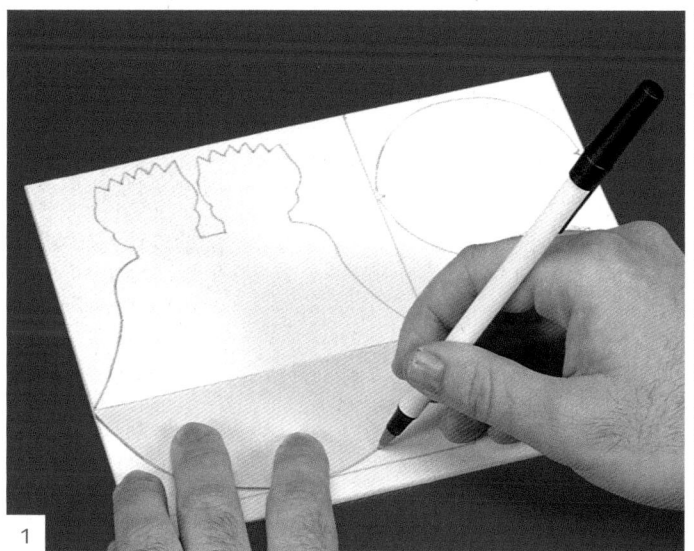

1

2

✱ *I recommend using a pencil to trace the patterns on the sheet foam. A nonpermanent pen or marker may smear when you color the puppet.*

T*iP

**1** On a piece of sheet foam, trace the patterns from page 21 lightly with a pencil. First, trace the basic shapes of the face: two boxes, one for the face and one for the jaw, and a circle in a separate area for the mouth. Next, draw the face and jaw shape of the puppet. **2** Draw the face details of your Coaster Creature. Also draw a tongue and teeth inside the circular mouth area. Be creative and give the face some personality! **3** Color the pattern, using permanent markers. If you use markers that aren't permanent, the ink may smear on your hands.

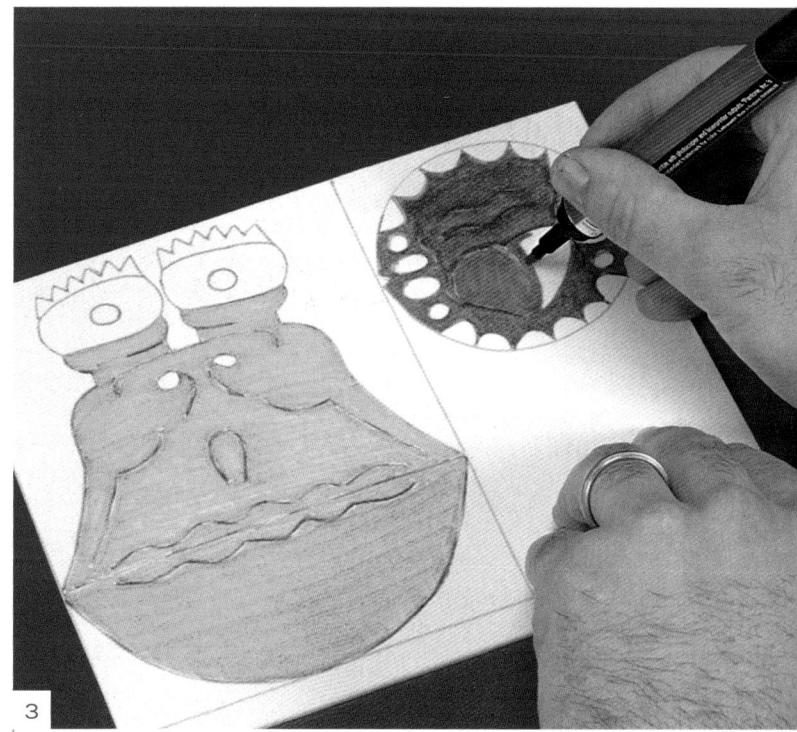

3

✱ *The pattern for this project gives you just a basic shape for a puppet face. You can draw your own Coaster Creature. Practice drawing on a piece of paper first, before you draw on the foam.*

T*iP

**4** Color the black areas (the eyes, eyelashes and nostrils) with a black permanent marker, then use the marker to darken all the lines of your Coaster Creature. **5** Cut out the pieces of the Coaster Creature with scissors. You should have three pieces when you finish: the jaw, the face and the mouth. Make sure you cut out the small notches on the mouth, as this will help you in gluing and folding the mouth. **6** You'll glue the jaw on the mouth first. Make a line of glue with the glue gun around the cut edge of the foam mouth where the jaw will attach, using the notches in the pattern to mark where the jaw will go. Once you finish gluing, attach the jaw carefully to the mouth. You will have to hold it as the glue dries. Next, apply the glue on the other side of the mouth for the face, using the notches in the pattern as a guide. There should be a little space between the corners of the jaw and face, which now surround the foam mouth. **7** Put your hand on the back of the mouth and squeeze to make the puppet's mouth close. Set the creature on its mouth to use it as a coaster.

## COASTER CREATURE **GAME**

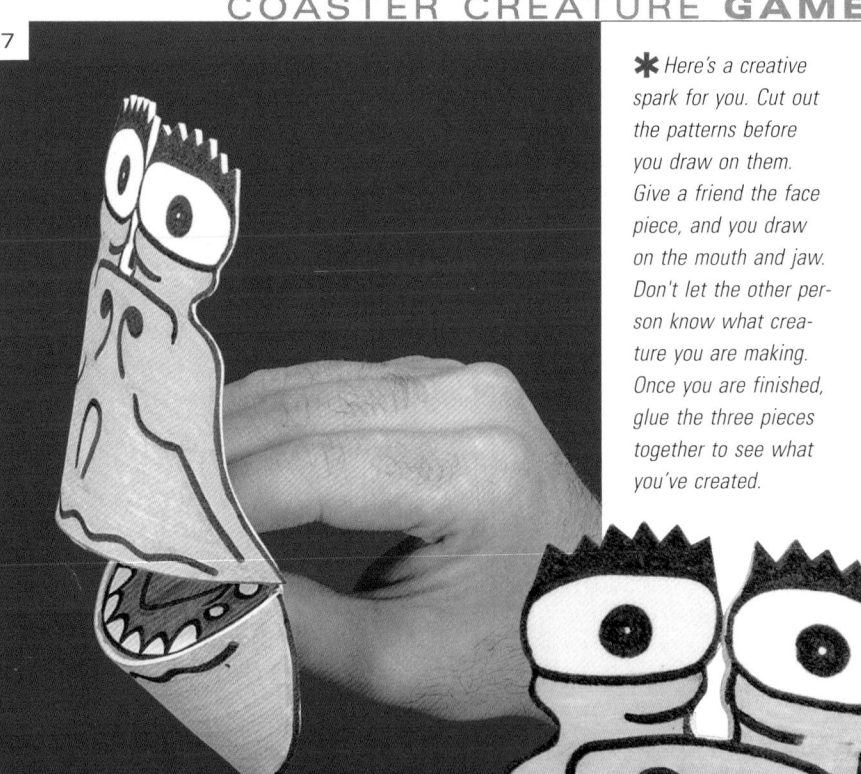

✱ *Here's a creative spark for you. Cut out the patterns before you draw on them. Give a friend the face piece, and you draw on the mouth and jaw. Don't let the other person know what creature you are making. Once you are finished, glue the three pieces together to see what you've created.*

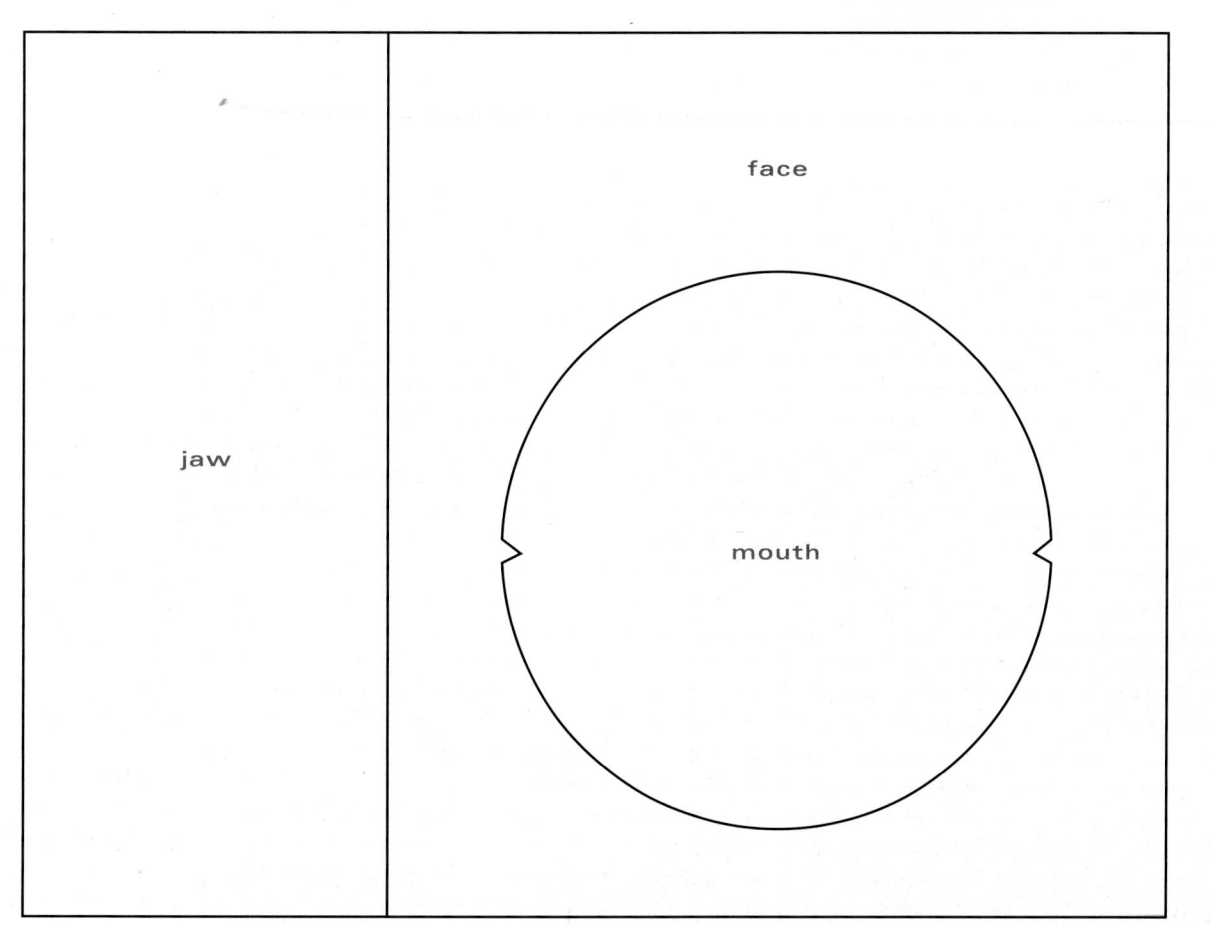

## Make More Puppets!

There's no limit to the number of Coaster Creatures you can make. Look for people around you who would make a good Coaster Creature. Find an interesting facial feature and make it the focus of the puppet's personality, or just make a funny face. Let your imagination go wild!

**THESE PATTERNS APPEAR AT FULL SIZE.**

face

jaw

mouth

MATERIALS

dishwashing liquid bottle

water bottle

two metal brads

black glove

two 1" (25mm) white pom-poms

two ½" (13mm) black pom-poms

black permanent marker

acrylic paint:
purple, yellow, blue and red

paintbrush

scissors

glue gun or craft glue

# BOTTLE BUG

**puppet 2** ▶

I like to think of Bottle Bug as a three-dimensional animated cartoon. To make a cartoon, a black-and-white drawing is copied onto a clear sheet of plastic. This creates a black outline of the drawing, and is called an animation cel. An artist then paints the different colors inside the black lines on the back of the cel. When thousands of such drawings, each showing a slight bit of movement, are copied, painted and then photographed with a movie camera, the image appears to move in real time.

With the Bottle Bug, a clear bottle is like an animation cel that has a black line drawing on top and paint on the inside. Just add a glove as the legs and you have a living cartoon!

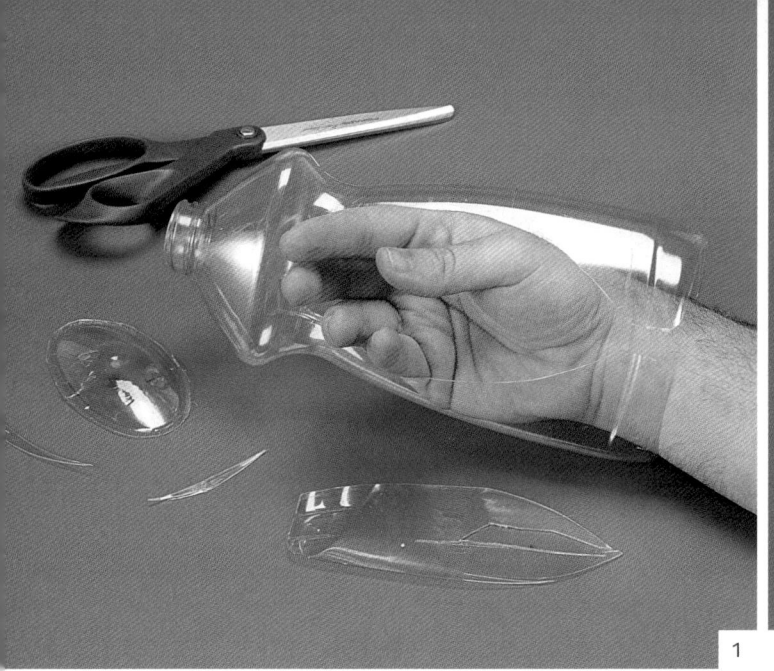

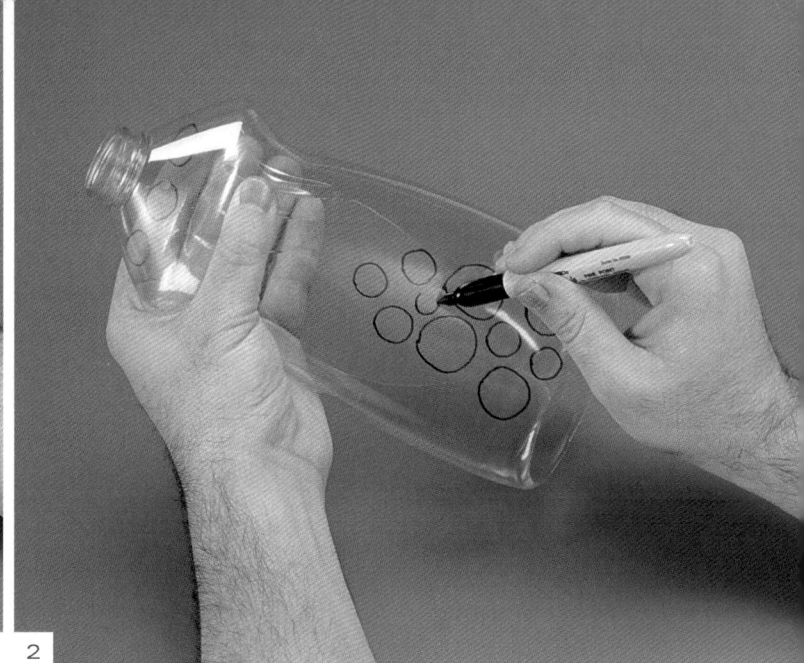

**1** Cut two holes in the dishwashing liquid bottle, one in the bottom and one on a flat side. Make sure you don't cut the bottle in half! Put your hand through the hole in the bottom of the bottle and then through the hole in the side, making sure the holes are big enough for your hand. If you have to, make the holes a little larger. **2** The dishwashing liquid bottle will be the body of your bug. Decide what color and design you want the bug to have, then draw the design on the plastic body of the bug with a black permanent marker. **3** Paint the inside of the bottle through the holes you just made. Use your marks as a guide. It may require several coats to paint the bug. Make sure each color is dry before you start another coat. **4** Cut the top and bottom off the water bottle, then cut the bottle in half lengthwise. Take one half, which will be the wings, and cut another line lengthwise through the center. Don't cut the wings completely apart. When you get 1" (25mm) from the top, stop and make a small U-shaped cut. This cut will keep the plastic from splitting when you spread the wings.

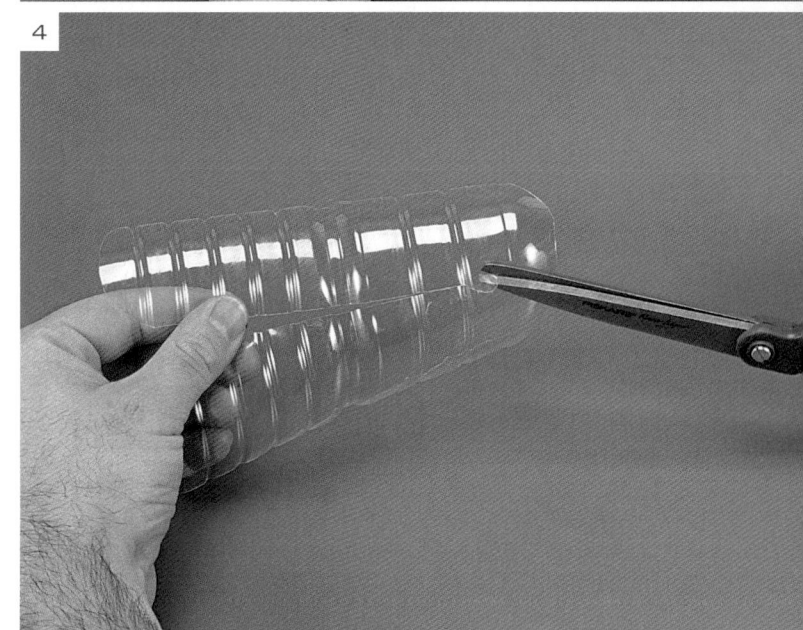

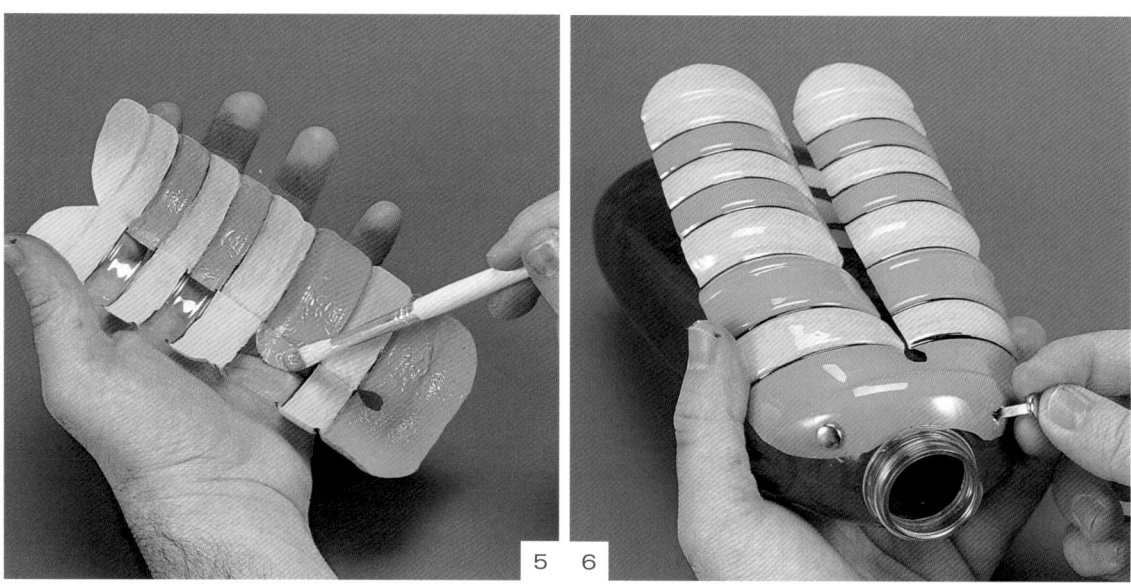

**5** Paint the wings the same way you did the body. Create a design on the outside with the marker, then use acrylic paints on the inside of the plastic. **6** Line up the wings of the bug on the back of the bug body. Once you have them lined up, make a hole near the top of each wing with scissors, then make a matching hole on the body of the bug. Attach the wings with a brad in each hole. If making a hole messes up the paint, you might have to go back and touch up the spot. **7** Glue the 1" (25mm) white pom-poms for the eyes above the bottle top. Glue on the ½" (13mm) black pom-poms for the pupils. Then paint the inside of the bottle top red for the mouth. **8** Put on the glove and stick your hand through the opening at the bottle bottom. Your fingers become the legs of the bug.

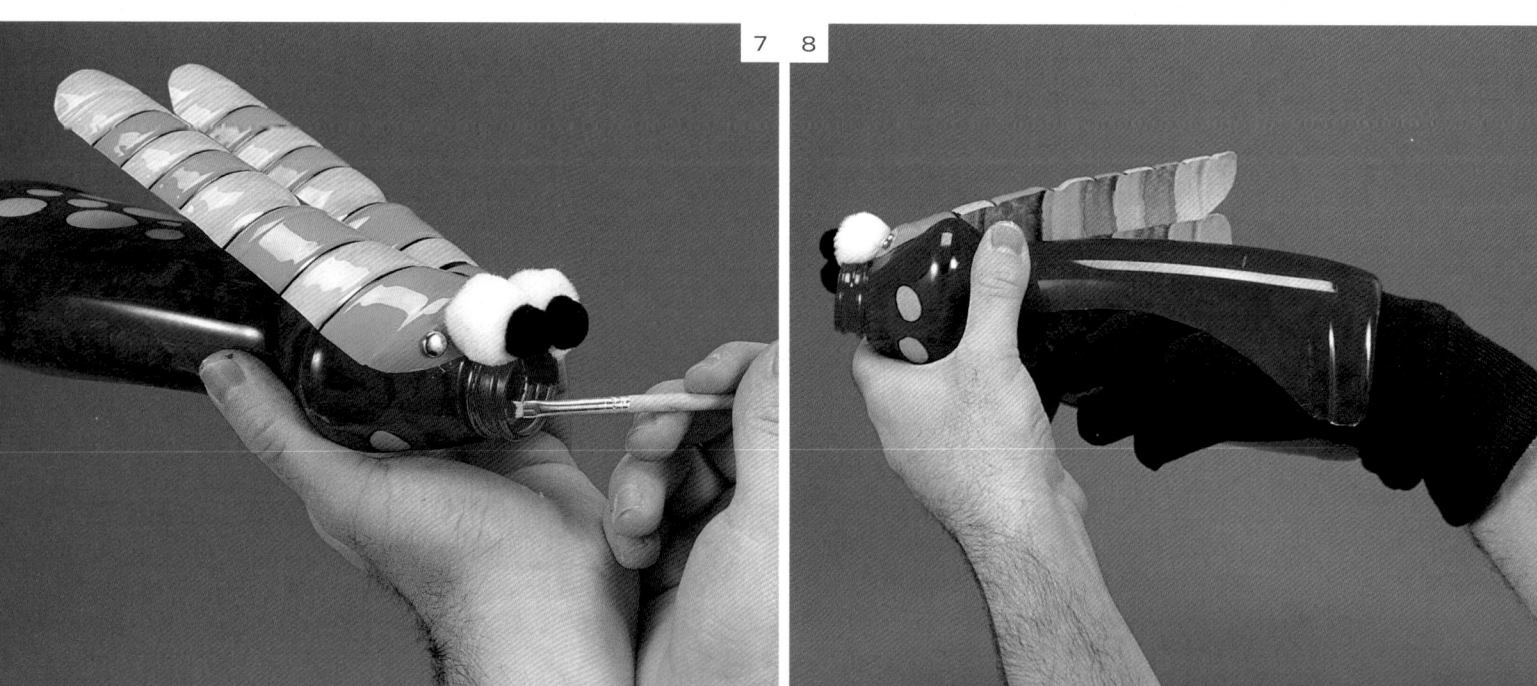

**9** Move your fingers to make the legs of the bug move.

9

Make More Puppets! Almost any kind of bottle could be a Bottle Bug. Water, soda pop, laundry detergent, fruit juice bottles and bowls are just a few possibilities. The design of the bug and the way you move your fingers will give the puppet personality. Adding antenna, a different face or a different design will also help create the Bottle Bug's unique style.

MATERIALS

tube sock

3½" (9cm) square of posterboard

3" x 4" (8cm x 10cm) piece of fur

3" x 5" (8cm x 13cm) piece of batting

3" (8cm) square of red felt

two ⅜" (10mm) black pom-poms

1" (25mm) black pom-pom

two 1" (25mm) white pom-poms

sixteen ½" (13mm) brown pom-poms

1" x 3" (25mm x 8cm)
piece of pink sheet foam

black permanent marker

scissors

glue gun

# SOCK PUPPY

**puppet** 3 ▶

After I graduated from high school, I did artist-in-residence workshops for elementary schools in Indiana. Sock puppets were some of the kids' favorites to make, and Sock Puppy became my faithful sidekick. He would lead a series of short skits that the kids performed as part of a big show for their parents.

Once, a child in the audience told me Sock Puppy wasn't real. I had to put my skills to the test. Without having to say a word, Sock Puppy acted his little heart out for over ten minutes. The audience was rolling with laughter. He made a believer out of that child, and the crowd loved him after that.

TIP

 *For this project you can use craft glue instead of a hot glue gun. It will work just as well.*

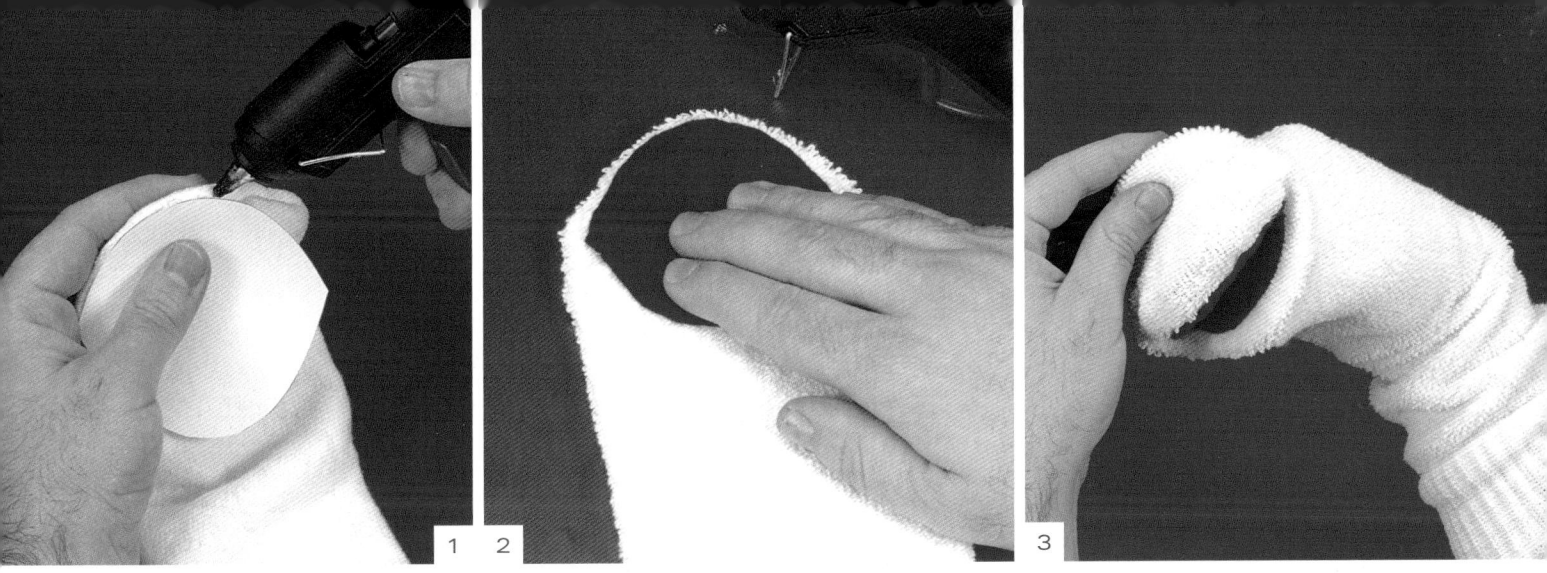

1

2

3

**1** Trace and cut out the posterboard mouth, the sheet foam tongue, the felt mouth and the fur ears from the patterns on page 29. Attach the posterboard mouth to the toe of the sock: glue the sock tip, then roll the edge of the sock and press it against the posterboard. The sock should not hang over the edge of the posterboard, and the seam of the sock should be hidden. Once you have the edge glued down, glue the rest of the posterboard against the sock. Let the glue dry. **2** Reach inside the sock and turn it inside out, so the posterboard is on the inside. Smooth the red felt mouth and make sure there are no wrinkles, then glue it over the seam at the toe of the sock and over the piece of posterboard inside the sock. Make sure the red felt covers the seam of the sock! **3** Take your piece of batting, roll it in half and use a spot of glue to help it keep its shape. Then push the batting into the sock, but not all the way to the end. Put your hand in the sock and bend the posterboard mouth in half. Push the batting so that it rests on top of your fingers when the mouth is closed, and not on the poster board.

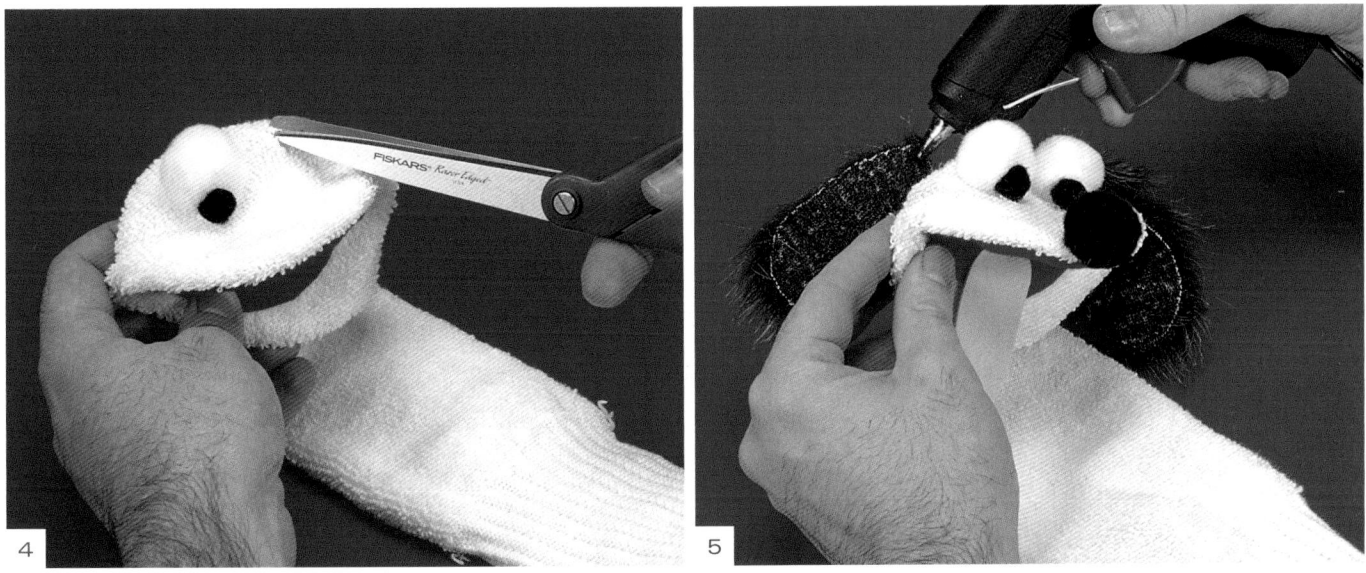

4

5

**4** The 1" (25mm) white and ⅜"(10mm) black pom-poms are the eyes. Decide where your eyes will be on the sock and make a small cut to mark each place. The eyes should be against the batting. Glue a white pom-pom in each mark, making sure to glue it to both the batting and the sock. Then glue the black pupils in place to finish the eyes. **5** The big black pom-pom will be the nose. Glue on the nose at the end of the mouth. Next, glue in the tongue. Just a spot of glue on the end of the tongue inside the mouth will work. Finally, glue on the fur ears behind the eyes.

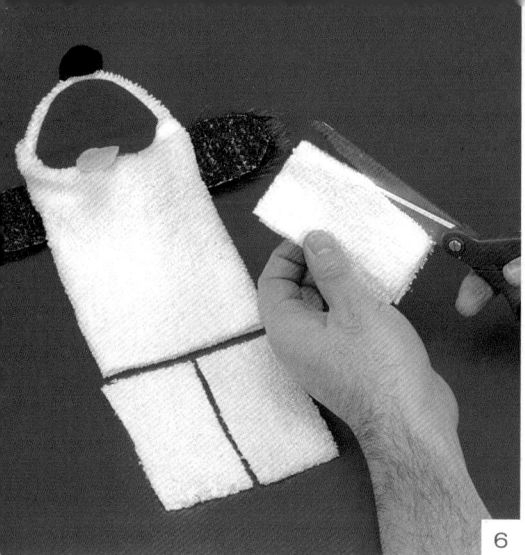
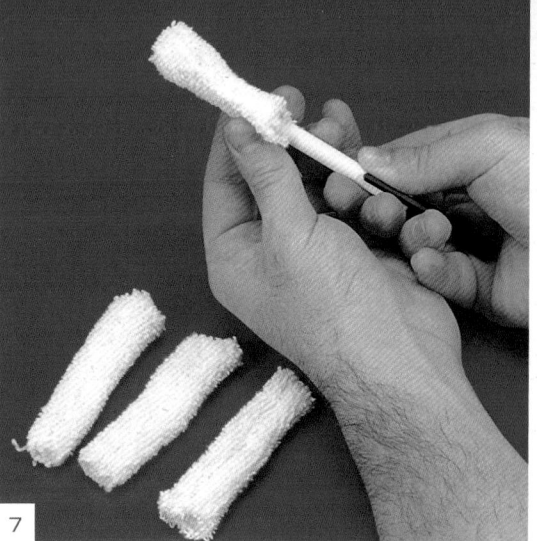
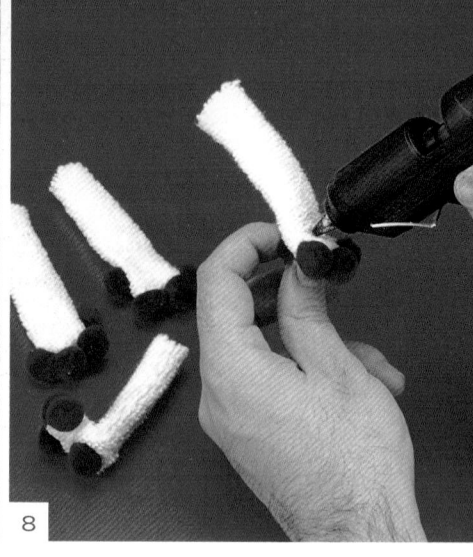

6 7    8

**6** Cut the elastic from the sock and discard it. Then cut about 2½" (6cm) from the bottom of the sock. Cut this piece into four equal-sized pieces. This will become the arms and legs. If your sock is longer or shorter, you might have to change the lengths or even cut the arms and legs from another sock. **7** With the smooth side up, apply glue to the one long edge of each sock piece, then roll the sock piece over to make a small tube. When dry, turn each rolled sock piece inside out so the fuzzy side is out. You can use a pen or pencil to help push the sock pieces inside out. **8** Use the brown pom-poms for the paw pads. For each arm, glue three pom-poms at the end, and then one a little further up the arm. Make sure the seam is on the inside. For each leg, glue three pom-poms on the end, and one pom-pom on the back of the leg. Then put a spot of glue about ½" (13mm) up the leg and fold the leg over. This will create a bend in the leg. **9** Glue the arms and legs on the puppet. The arms go beside the corner of the mouth on either side of the body. Glue the legs on the bottom of the sock, on the outside. **10** Put your hand into the bottom of the puppet and move the lips to make it talk.

☆
## Puppeteering Secret #6

Need some help performing with Sock Puppy? Turn to pages 10–12 to see Sock Puppy get emotional.

9    10

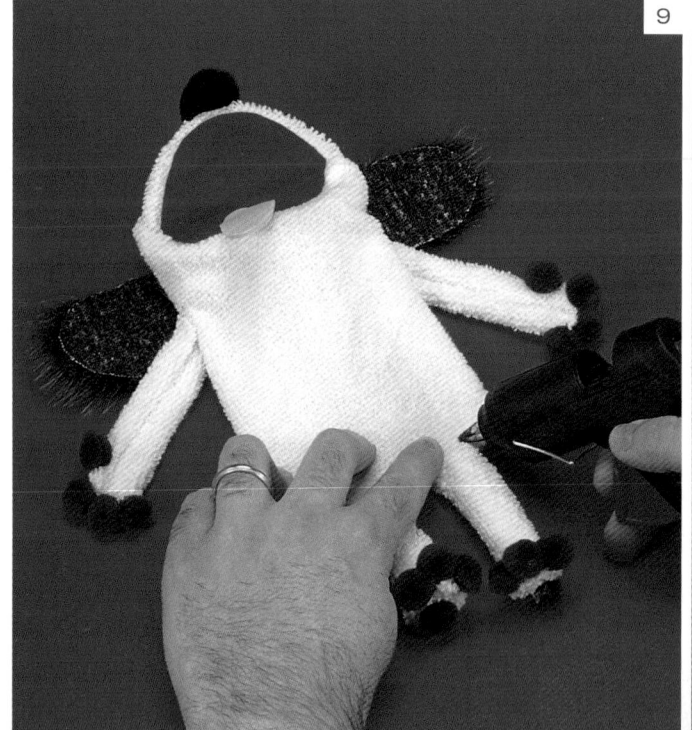

## Make More Puppets!

One way to get Sock Puppy to the stage is to write a melodrama for several of Sock Puppy's friends. For example, Sock Puppy might have to rescue the beautiful Miss Poodle from the Dastardly Dalmatian. You can imagine the perils Sock Puppy must face to free our heroine and see that justice is served!

THESE PATTERNS APPEAR AT FULL SIZE.

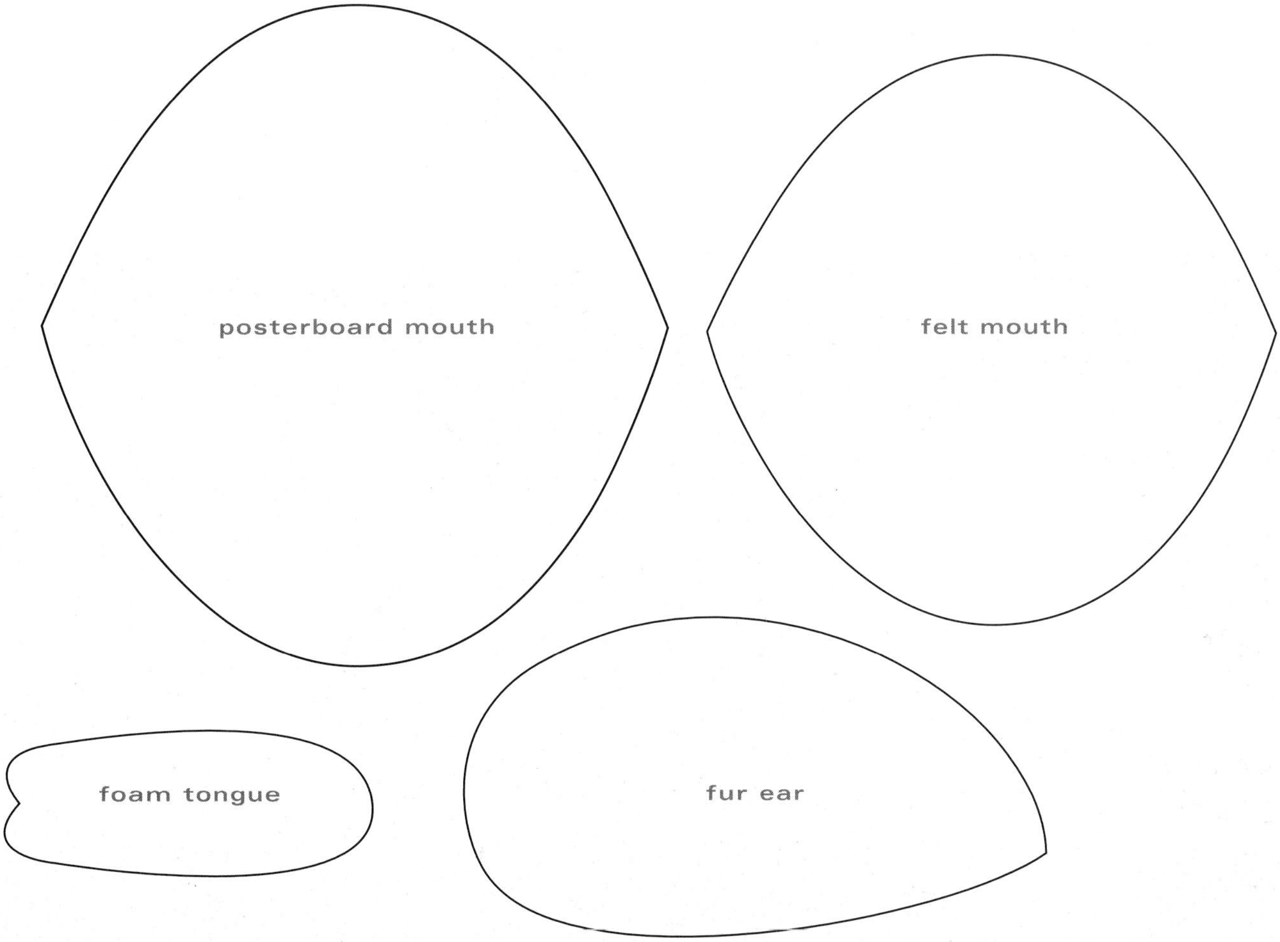

posterboard mouth

felt mouth

foam tongue

fur ear

12" (30cm) stuffed bear

5" x 7" (13cm x 18cm)
sheet of red foam

pencil

scissors

glue gun

# CONVERT-A-BEAR

**puppet 4** ▶

When I was in junior high school, I began a study of teddy bear patterns. I tore apart stuffed bears to see how they were made. The result was my own pattern that I could make on my mom's sewing machine. As you can imagine, it didn't take me long to turn my pattern into a series of different puppets. My favorites were a dog named Art and a bunny named Bongo. I still bring Bongo whenever I'm performing at a benefit.

Convert-a-Bear is a quick and easy way to make an adorable puppet from a stuffed doll that can meet and greet people at any event. It's also an affordable way for aspiring ventriloquists to practice the art of throwing their voice.

**TIP**

✳ *This project will completely remake your teddy bear! You can find inexpensive bears ready to make into puppets in just about any craft store.*

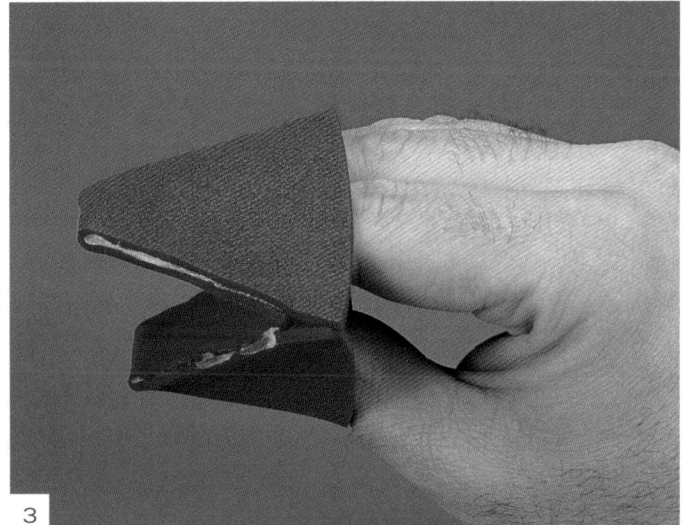

**1** Trace and cut out the mouth pattern on page 33 from a sheet of red foam. **2** Glue the mouth together. Start by gluing along the outside edge of the middle diamond and bringing the lower triangle up to attach the edges. Glue the other side the same way, so that you make a mouth shape. **3** When you are finished, make sure the mouth fits your hand and that all the glued edges are secure. **4** Use scissors to make a 4" (10cm) horizontal cut along the mouth of the bear. The cut should be centered under the nose of the bear.

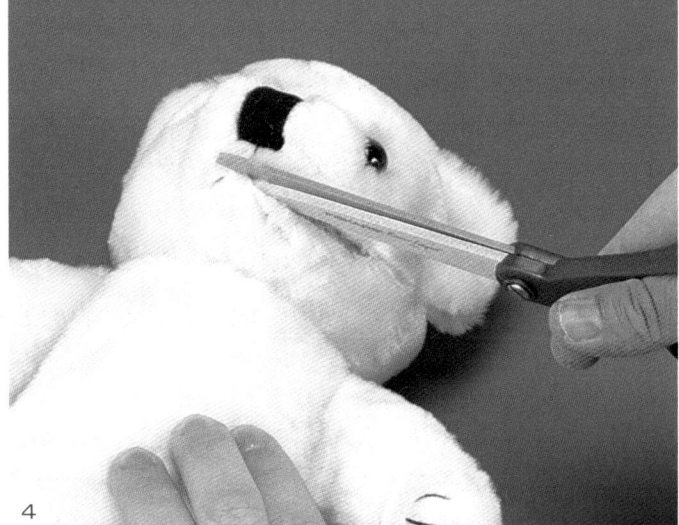

✳ *You might have to adjust the size of your cuts or the size of the pattern to fit your stuffed bear.*

TiP

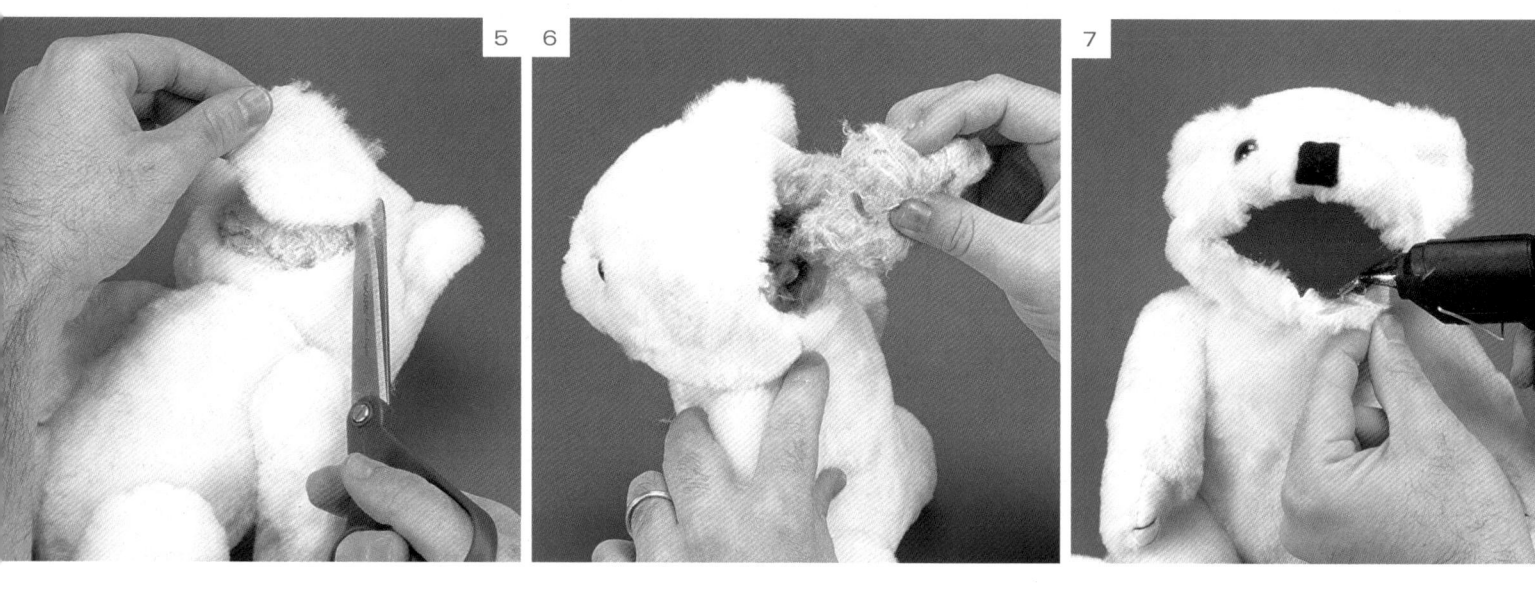

**5** Cut a 2" (5cm) diameter circle out of the back of the bear's head. **6** Pull some stuffing out of the back of the bear's head. Make sure you leave enough stuffing in the head and nose of the bear to keep their shape. Most of what you pull out should be from the mouth area. **7** Push the red foam mouthpiece through the hole in the back of the head and into the bear's mouth. The edge of the foam mouth should touch the edge of the cut you made. Use scissors to adjust the slit to fit the foam if necessary. Glue the edge of the fur to the rim of the mouth, starting under the nose and working around the lips. Apply the glue to the foam mouth and then press the fur of the bear to it, making sure to press inward so none of the inside stuffing of the bear shows. **8** Glue the back opening of the bear to the back of the mouth. Tuck all the stuffing into the bear, and as you glue, roll the bear's material inward to keep the cut edge from fraying. **9** Dress the bear as you like.

## TIP

✳ *If the stitching of the nose is lost when you pull out the stuffing, glue the nose back in place or add a black pom-pom for the nose.*

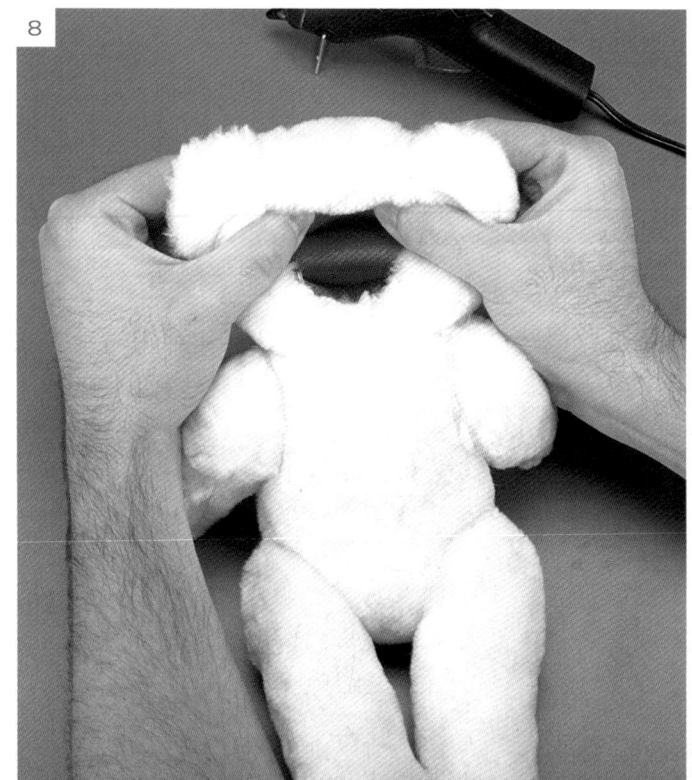

## Make More Puppets!

Just about any stuffed doll can be made into a puppet with a little imagination and the mouth pattern. After that, some clothes, accessories and a good personality are all you need to make a great character for your show.

PATTERN APPEARS AT FULL SIZE.

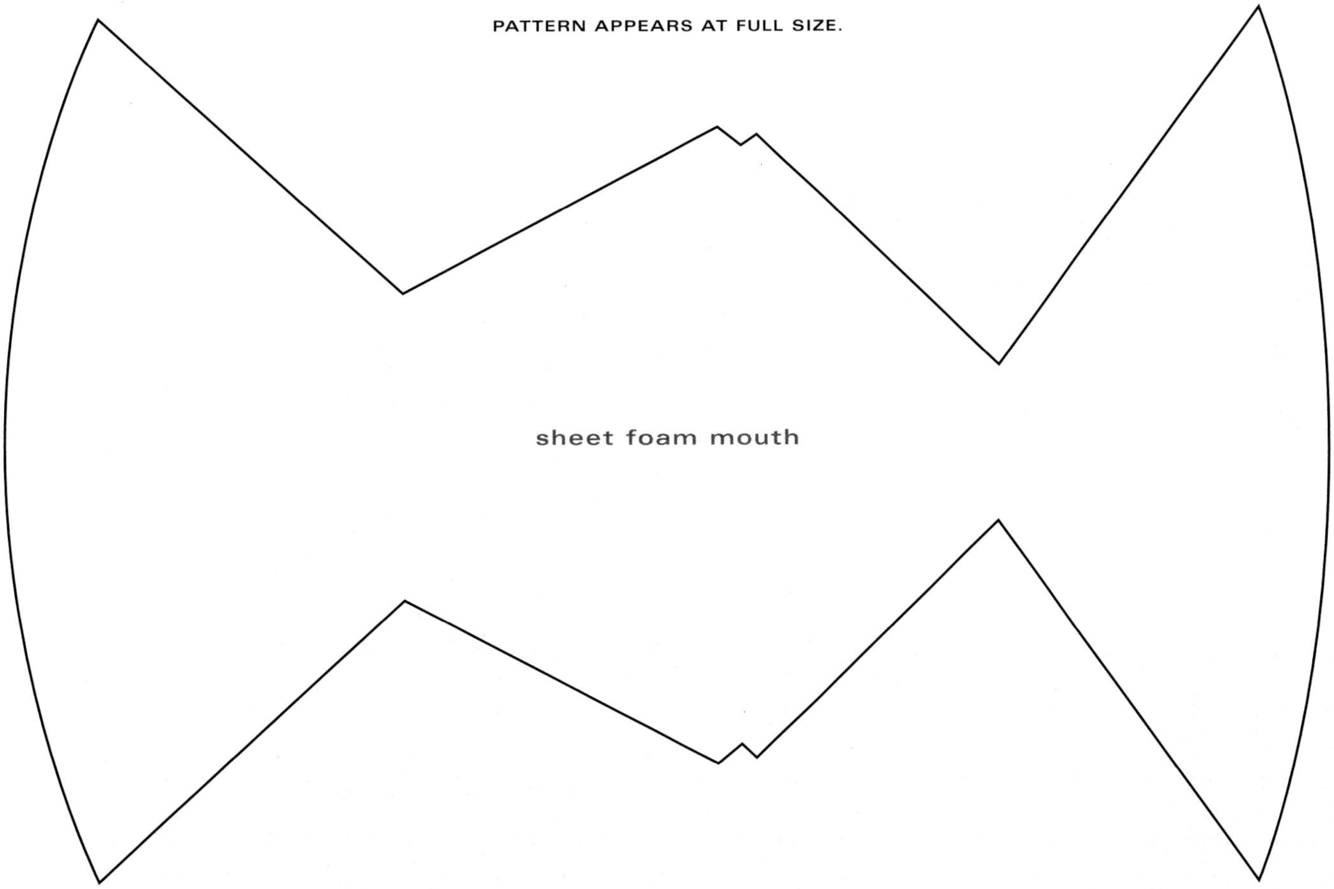

sheet foam mouth

## MATERIALS

green tube sock
*(you may have to dye it)*

two-liter plastic bottle

3½" (9cm) square of posterboard

3" (8cm) square of red felt

3" x 5" (8cm x 13cm)
strip of batting

1" x 5" (3cm x 13cm)
strip of black felt

two wooden half apples

two plastic jewels

two 9" x 11" (23cm x 28cm)
sheets of felt: one brown
and one green

black permanent marker

pencil

scissors

glue gun

# SOCK TURTLE

**puppet 5** ▶ A puppeteer friend of mine who was working at a theme park once asked me to build him a fun puppet that he could carry around as he led park tours. The park had a water theme, so I made him a turtle that could pop its head in and out of a shell. It was a big hit because the turtle could come out of its shell whenever it had a comment and duck back in when my friend had to speak.

Here's my cute little turtle. I've simplified it into a sock puppet but it still has that great peekaboo feature that surprises people.

* *Make sure the sock you choose for your turtle is long enough for the two-liter bottle after you cut off the elastic. You might have to make some adjustments to the bottle and the pattern.*

TIP

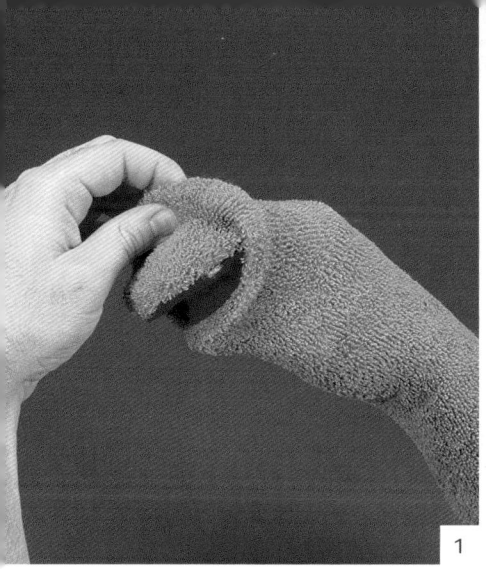
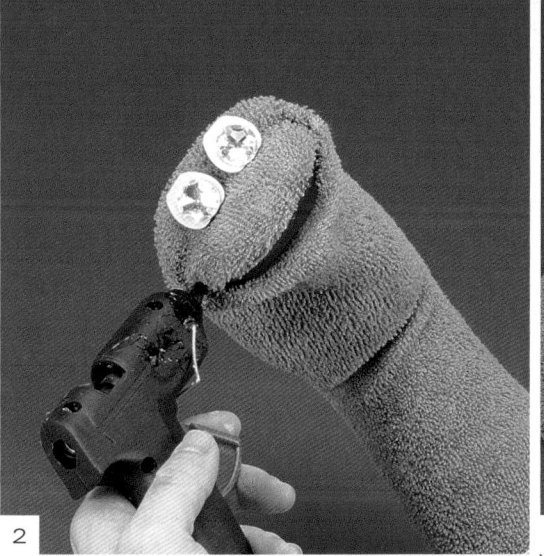
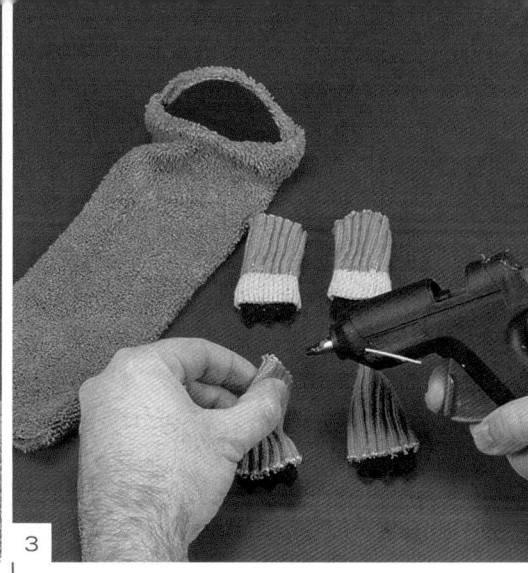

1 2 3

❋ *When you pinch the opposite ends of the back legs, pinch them perpendicular to the claw ends. They will tuck into the shell and make the turtle look like it's sitting.* TiP

**1** You will begin by making a sock puppet exactly like the Sock Puppy found on page 26. Trace and cut out the posterboard mouth and the red felt mouth from the Sock Puppy patterns on page 29, and the black felt claws from the Sock Turtle pattern on page 37. Glue the posterboard mouth on the end of the sock, then pull the sock inside out and glue on the red felt mouth. Next, roll up the batting, glue the ends and push it into the sock. Bend the mouth in half and move the batting so it sits on your hand when you close the mouth. **2** Next, attach the eyes by cutting a small slit in the sock where each eye will be and gluing the wooden half apples on both the batting and the sock. Glue plastic jewels as pupils on the half apples. You can also glue a smile on your turtle by rolling the sock forward near the mouth and gluing the rolled sock at the corners of the mouth. This creates the smile. **3** Cut the elastic end off the sock. Cut four equal lengths from the elastic. Roll the cut pieces and glue them together, then turn them inside out. Cut the claws out of black felt and glue them at the end of each piece. Pinch and glue closed the ends opposite the claws. **4** Cut off the bottom curved part of the plastic bottle. Then, use the marker to make two marks on opposite sides of the top of the bottle, just where the bottle starts to curve. Make a straight line between the marks on one side, and make a bell-shaped curve on the other side between the marks. Cut the top of the bottle along the line. **5** Glue the brown felt over the shorter half of the bottle first. This will be below the green shell, and you will need to cover a little more than half the bottle. Cut off the excess felt and save it for the pieces of the shell. Smooth the felt and make sure there are no lumps or folds. Fold the felt over the upper and lower edges and glue it inside the bottle.

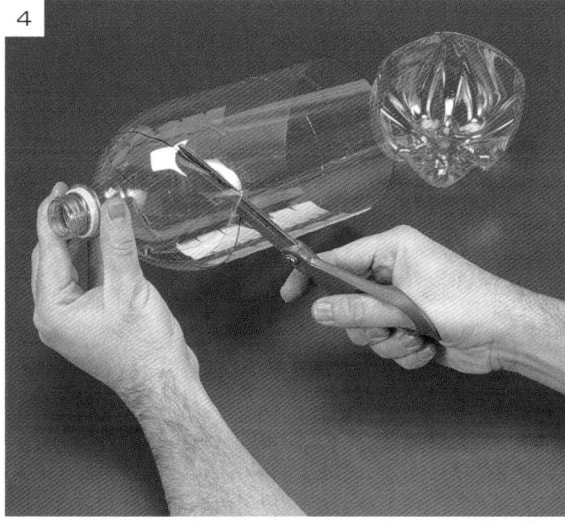

4

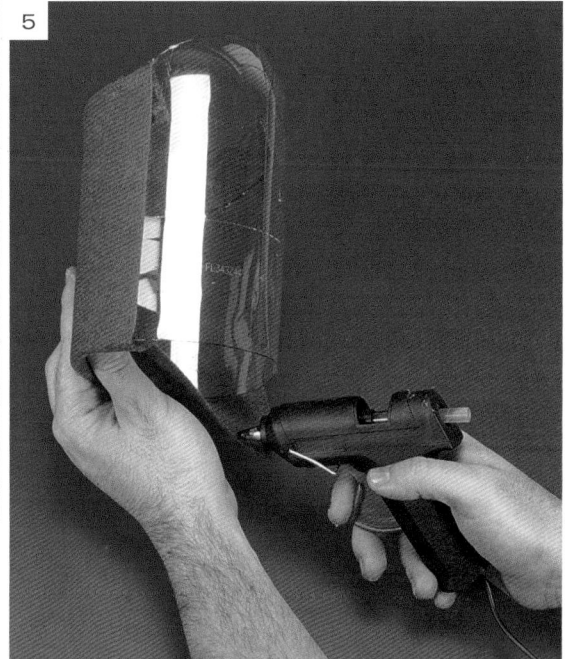

5

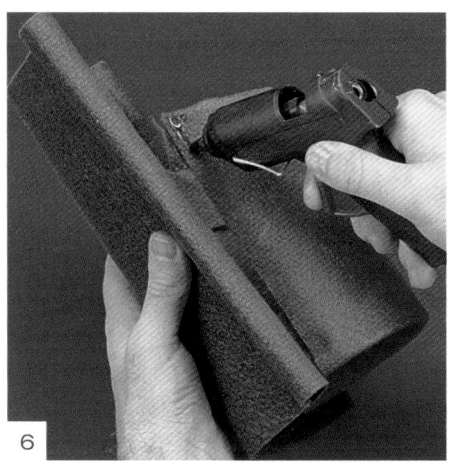
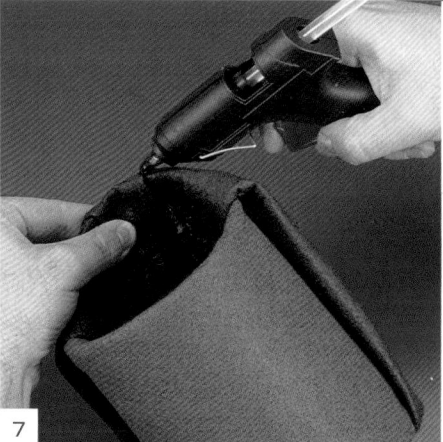

**TIP**

✱ *If you use a glue gun directly on the plastic bottle, the plastic may melt! When working on this project, apply glue to the felt and let it cool for a second before pressing it against the plastic bottle.*

**6** Add the green felt above the brown shell. For this part of the shell, you will fold over the excess felt instead of cutting it off. Position the felt on the top of the bottle so there's a 1" (25mm) overhang at the bottom. Fold the extra felt on the sides so the green felt overlaps the brown by about 1" (25mm). Glue the green felt to the brown; to do this, add glue to the brown felt and press the green in place. **7** Glue the bottom 1" (25mm) overhang inside the bottle. Glue the sides in first, then the middle. Now glue the top overhang the same way. There should be more extra felt at the top of the bottle than the bottom.

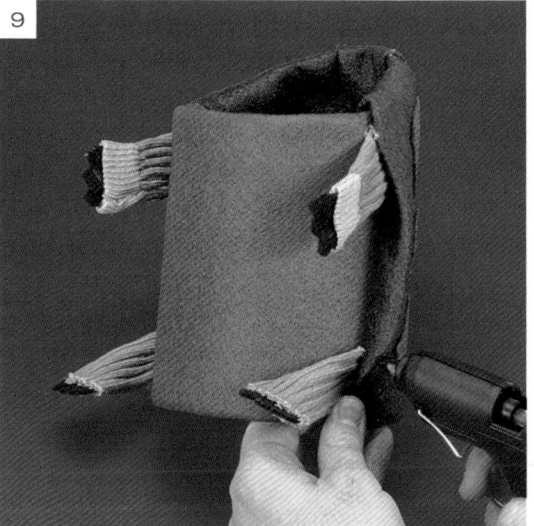
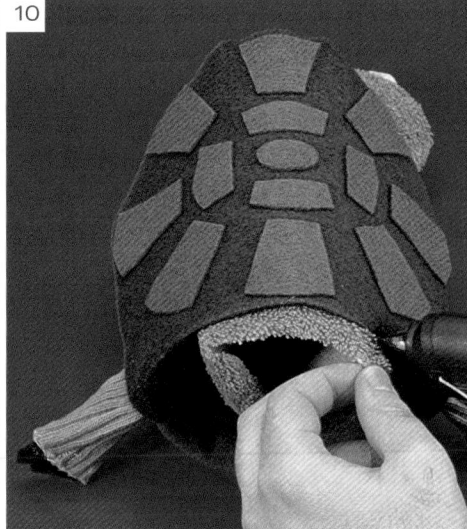

**8** Trace and cut out the shell plates from the leftover brown felt. Cut them in any shape you like, and then arrange them on the green shell. You can have as many or as few shell plates as you want, and you can create any pattern you like. **9** Glue the legs inside the folded edge of the green shell. **10** Put your hand in the sock puppet, and then through the bottle. Make sure the head extends through the top. Next, pull out your hand, leaving the sock behind, and put a line of glue on the bottom of the sock, about 1" (25mm) from the end. Apply the glued end to the bottom of the bottle, squeezing to make sure the sock holds in place and is centered beneath the shell.

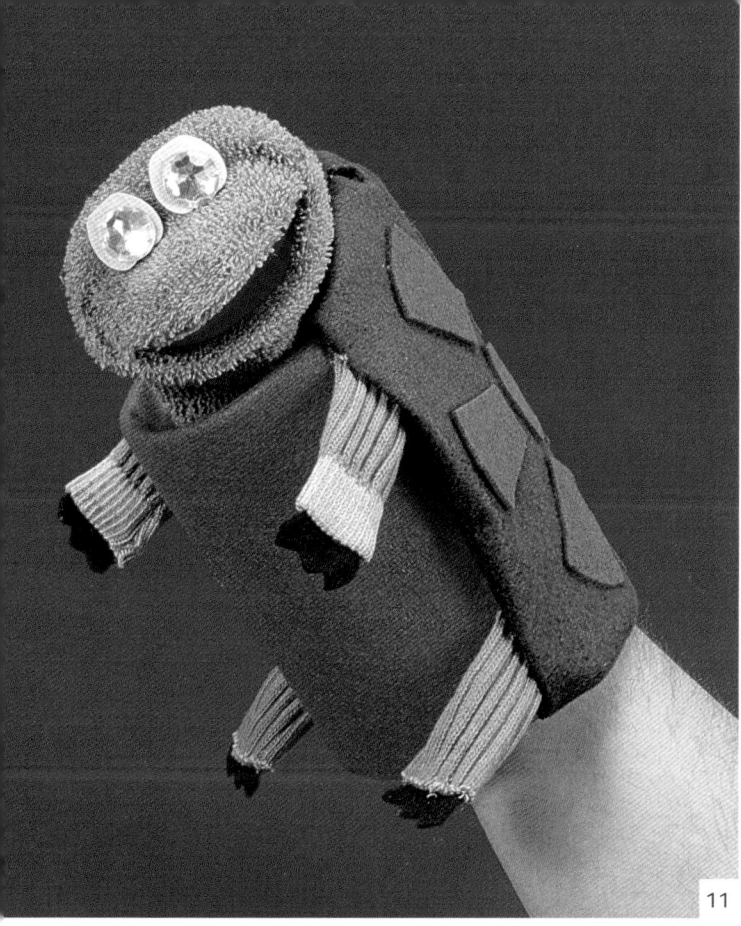

**11** Put your hand in the sock. You can pull your hand up and down in the bottle to extend or hide the head.

**THESE PATTERNS ARE ACTUAL SIZE**

## Make More Puppets!

Although real turtles can be dull in color, I like experimenting with bright color combinations for the Sock Turtle. Try different colored shell plates or beads and jewels for eyes. Add a little sparkle and you may find yourself coming out of your shell.

mouth

claws

one 10" x 4" (25cm x 10cm) piece
of 2" (5cm) thick foam rubber

six 3⁄16" (5mm) white pom poms

two 3⁄8" (10mm) white pom poms

two 3⁄16" (5mm) black pom poms

permanent black marker

pencil

scissors

glue

MATERIALS

# BANANA BUDDY

**puppet** **6** ▶

During my college days I did some work as a strolling puppeteer at the Indianapolis Union Station. I would set up and do a 10-minute show in the mall area right across from a gift shop that sold interesting artwork. I wanted to sell some squeeze-mouth foam animal puppets in the gift shop and call them the Foamy Farm. The Banana Buddy is a close relative to those foamy animal friends, but he doesn't need sculpted arms and legs. Who ever heard of a banana with arms and legs?

**✳ Yellowing Foam**

*Foam sheets are usually white. To make it yellow, you can either leave the foam in the sun until it yellows (or ripens!) or dye it yellow. A yellow permanent marker will work, as well.*

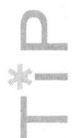

TIP

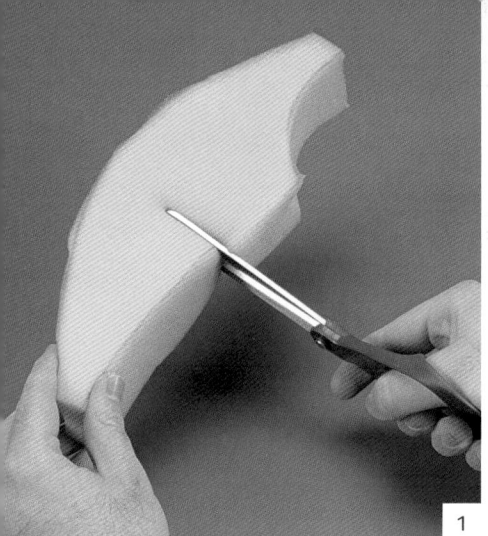
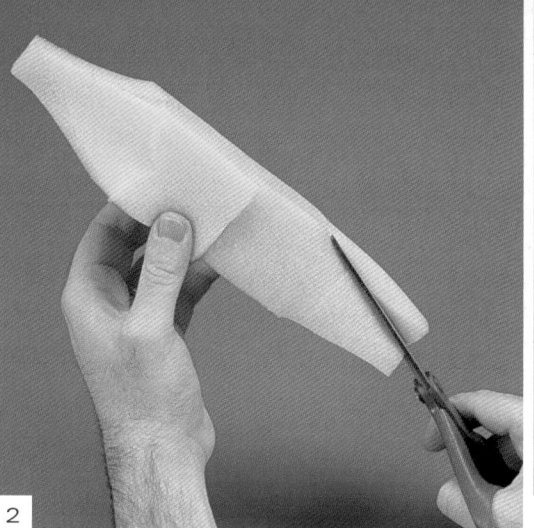
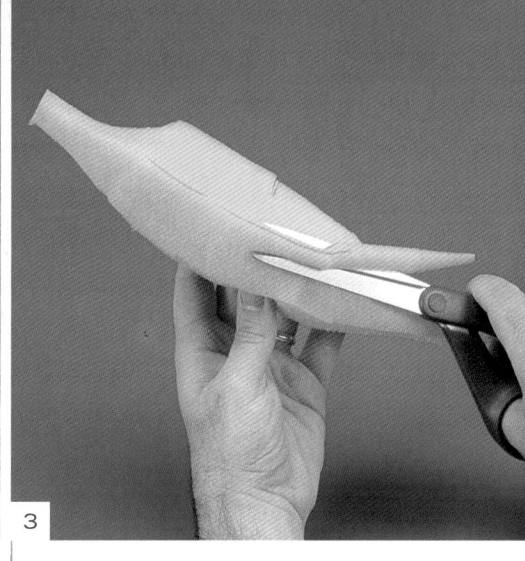

1 2

3

❋ Use sharp scissors and make long, clean cuts as you are cutting out your banana buddy. The less you have to adjust your scissors which each cut, the cleaner your peel panels will be. An electric carving knife is perfect for cutting out the pattern.

T*iP

**1** Trace the pattern from page 41 on the foam and cut it out using scissors. Then, with a single cut of the scissors, make a slit in the foam where the mouth should be on the banana. **2** Taper the top and bottom of the banana by making a single cut along the edge of each corner. You will need to make four cuts total, tapering the end of the banana almost to a point. **3** Continue tapering the edges on the top and bottom of the banana. Remember, bananas aren't square. Cut the corners near the face to make peel panels. **4** Make smaller cuts around the face to add facial details. First, cut up along the bridge of the nose. This will determine the angle of the nose. Next, cut down from where the eyebrows will be, meeting the last nose cut. You will remove a triangle of foam from the face of your banana. The higher the angle of the eyebrow cut, the happier your Banana Buddy will look.
**5** Next, create eye sockets by making two cuts, one angled up and one angled down, on either side of the nose. This will determine the width of the nose and the eye sockets.

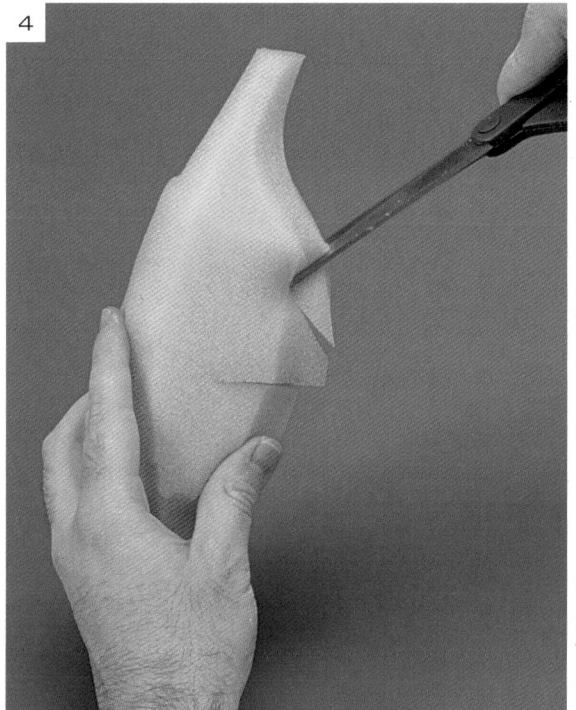
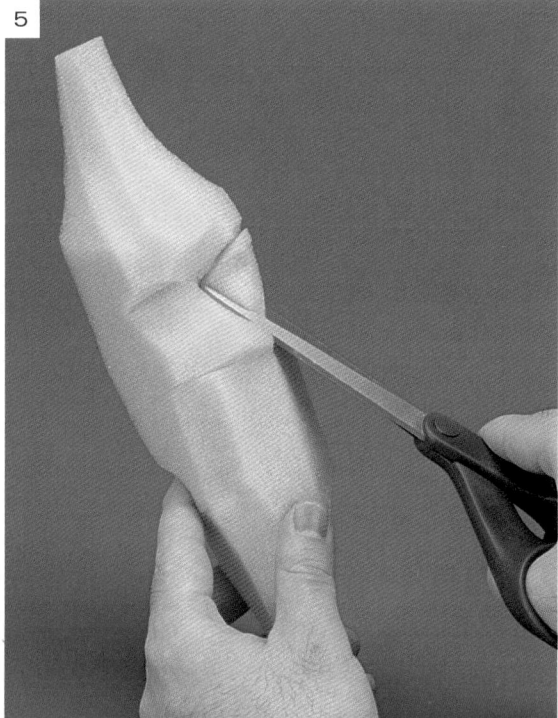

4

5

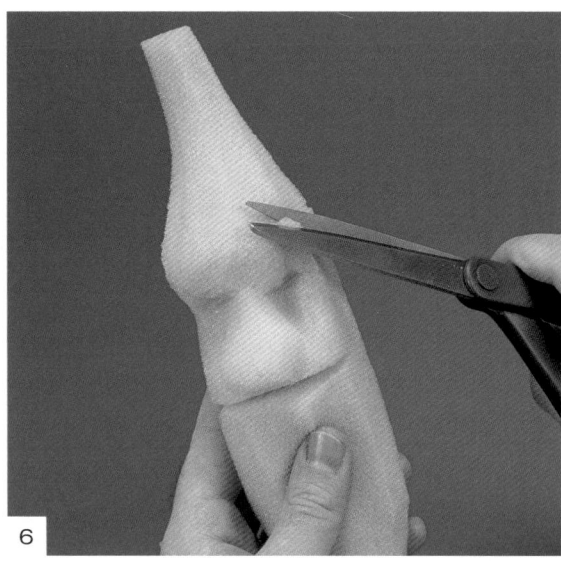

6

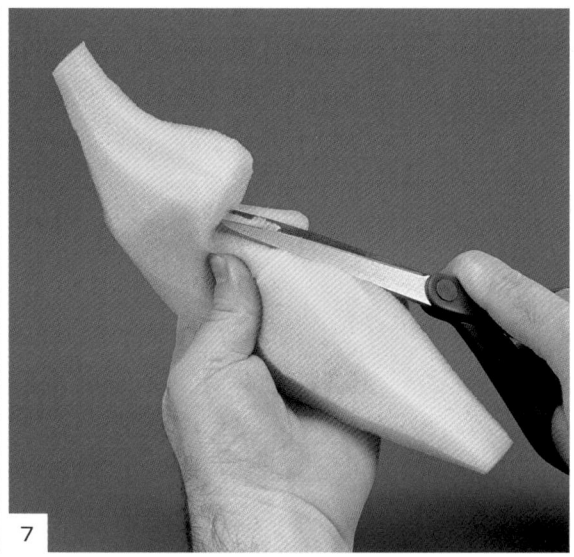

7

**6** You should now have a rough profile of the face, with the nose and eye sockets defined. Smooth the rough chunky edges of the Banana Buddy's face with little cuts with your scissors and round the edges carefully. There should be no need for big cuts at this point, just smoothing out the edges. **7** A good scissors cut you can make for a well-defined nose is a "divot" cut. Open your scissors just a little bit and press the tips into the side of the nose. Press deep, then make your cut. This will really give your nose definition and dimension. **8** Use a black permanent marker to shade in the mouth, the eye sockets, the eyebrows and the top and bottom tips of the banana. A good way to do this is to draw around the area you will color, then color it in. The longer you press the marker against the foam, the darker the mark will be. **9** Last, glue on the small white pom-poms for the teeth, the large white pom-poms for the eyes and the black pom poms for the pupils.

TiP

✳ *If you make a mistake with your black permanent marker, you can make corrections with your scissors. Just trim away the black marks.*

## SMOOTHING FOAM RUBBER

8   9

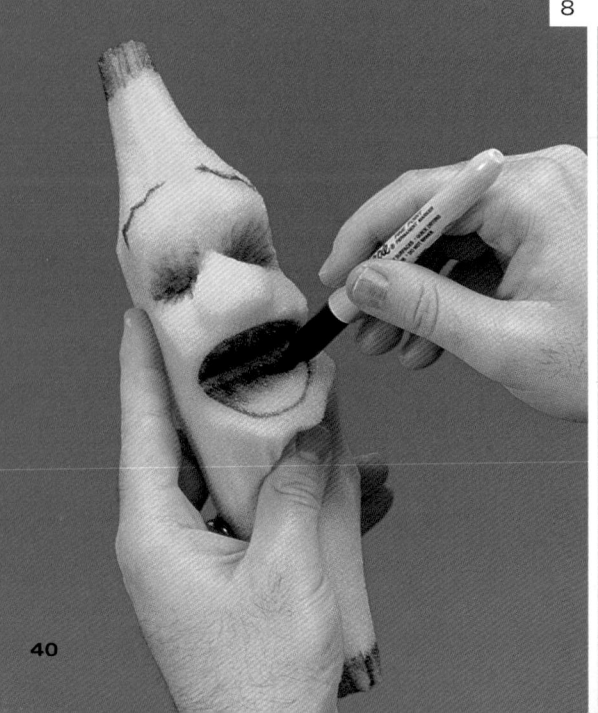

✳ *Smoothing is the art of snipping away the ridges of foam caused by making big cuts with your scissors. As you keep snipping each side of the cut on your foam puppet, the ridges get smaller and smaller until they smooth away.*

10

**10** Squeeze below the mouth to make your banana talk.

*❋* If you like, you can add eyebrows with a little piece of fur.

TiP

ENLARGE THE FOLLOWING PATTERN 125% FOR THE FOAM BANANA.

**Make More Puppets!** Coming up with a design for your Banana Buddy is a matter of personal preference. You can either pre-plan your character by sketching on paper and then converting the outlines to guide marks on the foam or simply let the scissors inspire you by making free-style cuts that will lead you to a completed character.

8½" x 11" (22cm x 28cm)
color portrait photo

6" x 7" (15cm x 18cm)
piece of poster board

red or black marker or colored pencil

pen

scissors

craft glue or glue stick

double-sided tape *(optional)*

# PICTURE PUPPET

**puppet** **7** ▶

I consider Picture Puppet a high-tech version of the Coaster Creature. There are a lot of great ways to use the Picture Puppet. If you know someone who is running for public office, the Picture Puppet is a perfect way to get that person's face out there. For a fun party idea, you can find the faces of your favorite actors and actresses in magazines and make color copies of them. You can act out scenes with your puppet cast. Another good idea is to make Picture Puppets of historical figures for a history project.

Of course, a Picture Puppet of a friend on their birthday makes a perfect gift.

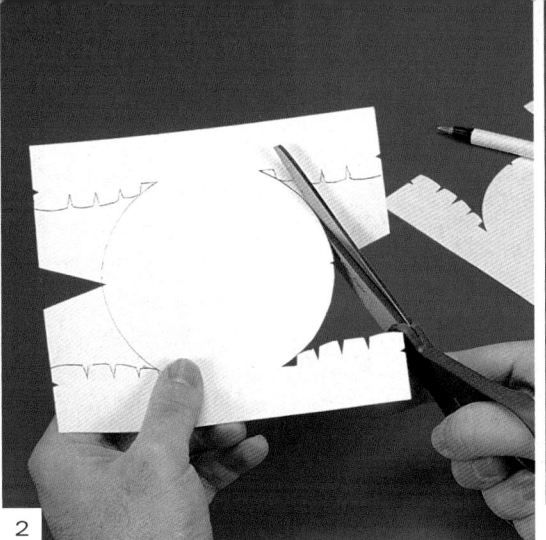
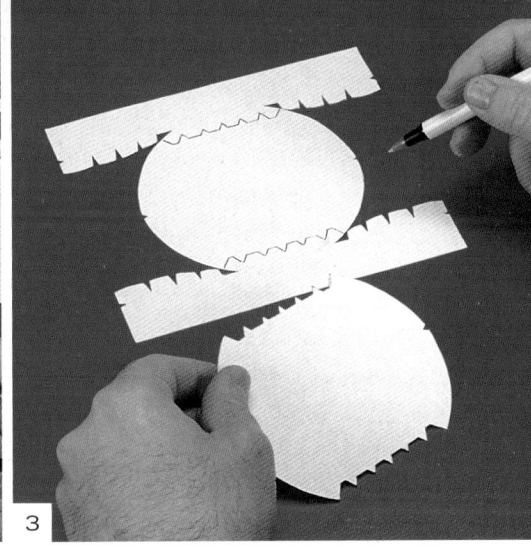

1    2        3

**1** Use a photocopier to enlarge the photo of a face you want to make into a puppet. The face should fill a 8½" x 11" (22cm x 28cm) color copy. If your picture is a different size, you might have to make some adjustments to the pattern. If you don't have a photo you can use, you can paint or draw one. **2** Trace and cut out the teeth on posterboard, using the pattern on page 45. Make sure you cut around all the teeth. **3** Line up the inner mouth pattern and the teeth at the notches. Use the inner mouth pattern to trace in the teeth on the mouth. **4** Color the inside of the mouth with a red or black marker or colored pencil. Do not color the teeth. **5** Bend all the teeth down, and then bend the top and bottom panels down, as well.

TIP

**✱** *You can also make the mouth color from red construction paper by tracing the inner mouth pattern on the construction paper and cutting it out with scissors. Make sure you cut around the teeth, then glue the construction paper in place by lining up the notches.*

4

5

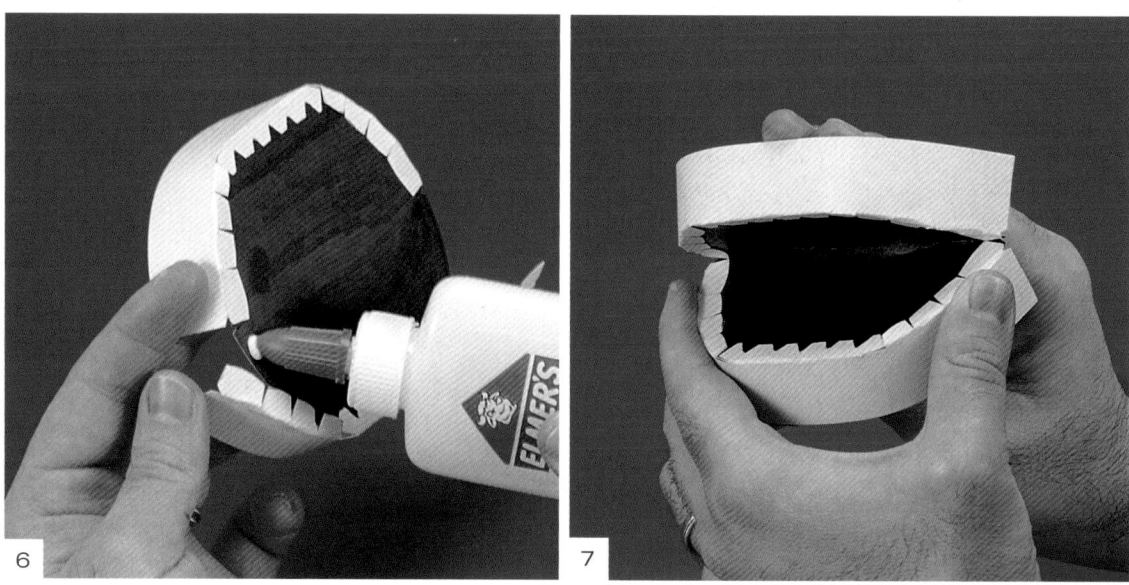

**6** Glue the teeth to the inside of the mouth, bending the panels around the inner mouth circle. It might help to glue the last tooth down first, and then glue down the rest of the teeth. **7** Fold the mouth carefully in half at the notches. **8** Cut out the face and trim the edges. Then cut straight across the center of the mouth. **9** Glue the lower and upper face pieces to the mouth, lining up the mouth on the edges. You could use double-sided tape to attach the picture, as well. **10** Clip off the exposed edges of the mouth piece. Make sure the edge of the mouth is even with the edge of the picture.

# TIP

✱ *When cutting out the mouth you can draw a line across the picture to help make sure your cut is straight.*

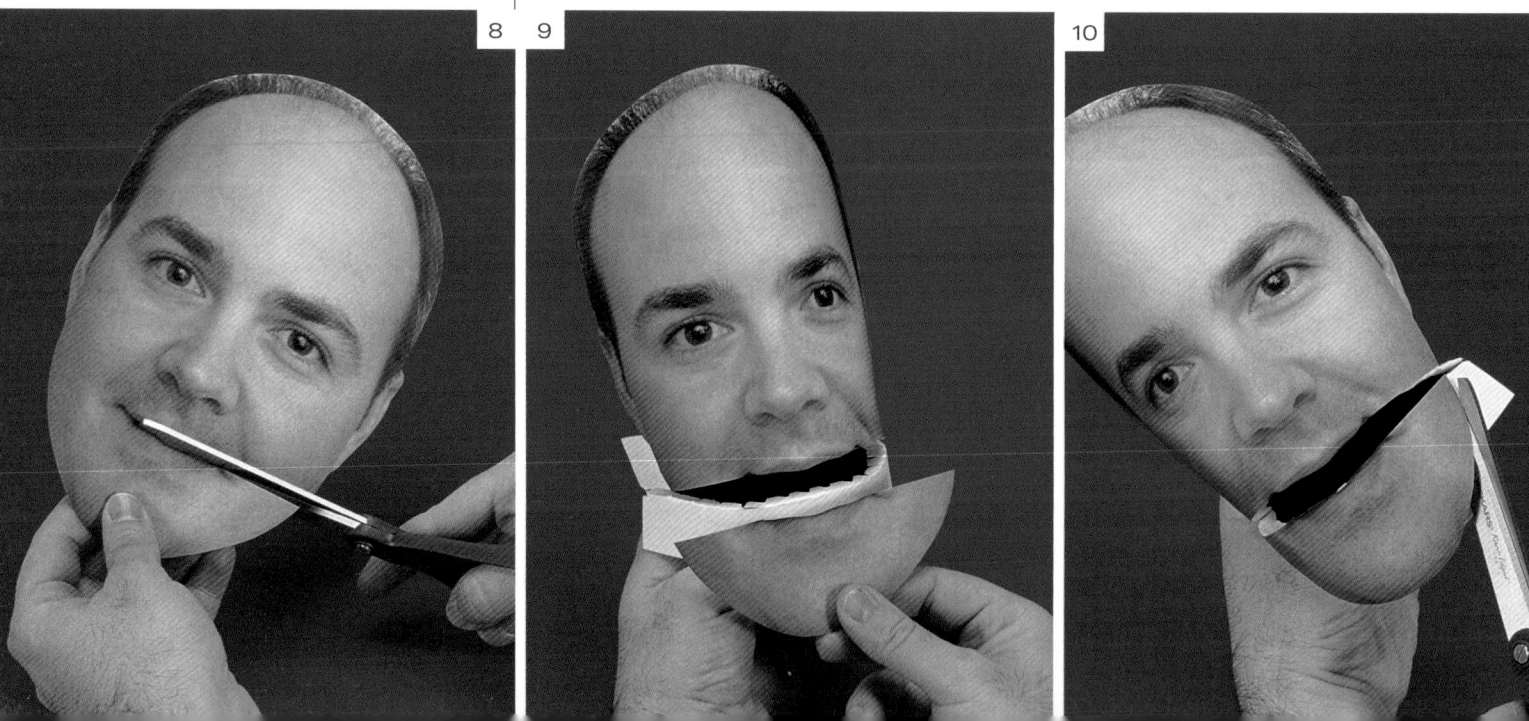

**11** If you have trouble gripping the puppet you can use double-sided tape on the mouthpiece where you grip the puppet.

☆
## Puppeteering
### Secret #7

The Picture Puppet can be a lot of fun in puppet shows. You can use it to do an impression of a famous person, or create one of someone in the audience. Or you can have a funny conversation with yourself during a performance!

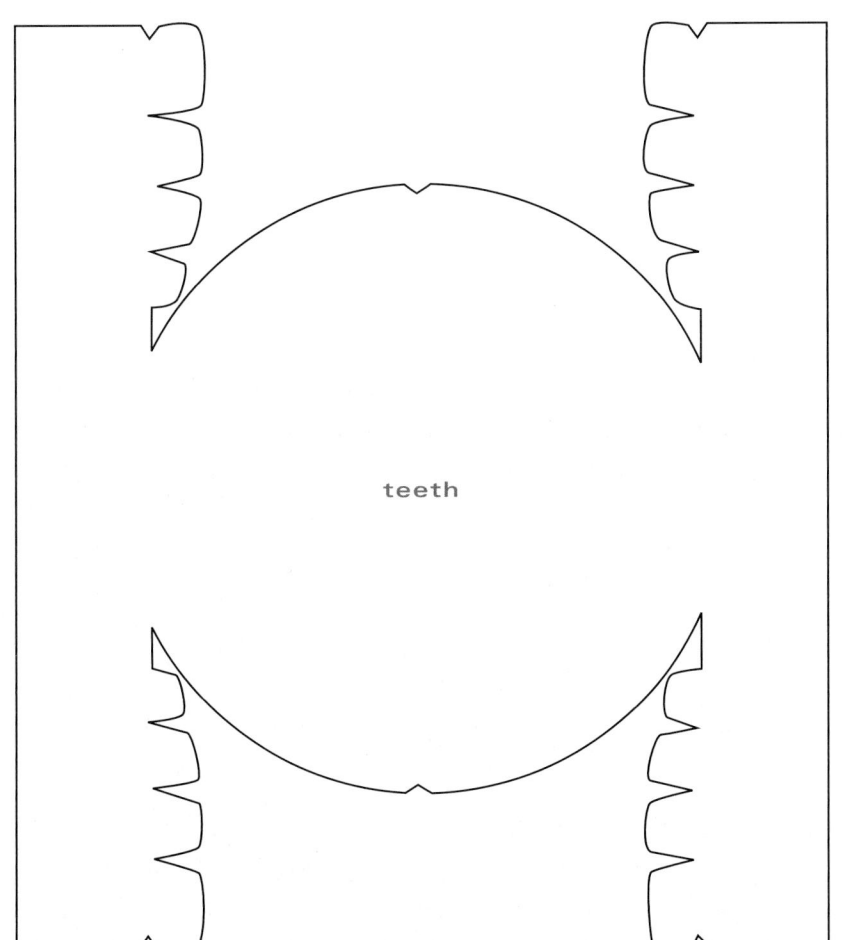

teeth

**ENLARGE THESE PATTERNS TO 125%.**

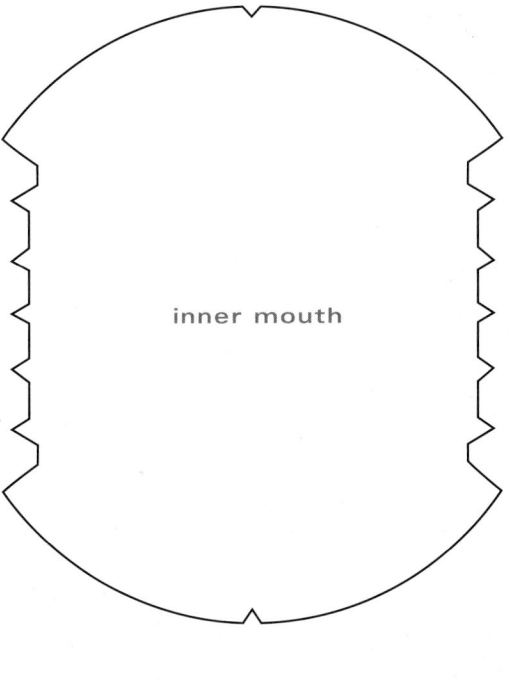

inner mouth

## MATERIALS

6" x 3¼" (15cm x 8cm) rectangle of 1" (25mm) thick foam rubber

12" (30cm) square of medium shag fur

3" x 4" (8cm x 10cm) sheet of brown felt

craft stick

one ¼" (6mm) pink pom-pom

sixteen ½" (13mm) tan pom-poms

two ¾" (18mm) white pom-poms

two 3⁄16" (5mm) black pom-poms

two ¾" (18mm) tan pom-poms

one 1" (25mm) white pom-pom

½" (13mm) square of white sheet foam

black permanent marker

scissors

glue gun

# RUNNING RABBIT

**puppet 8 ▶**

The Running Rabbit started his puppet life as a marionette, but tying the strings is complicated. I wasn't going to put him in this book, but at the last minute I remembered the story of the tortoise and the hare and thought his legs would be great for running. Even without the strings, this puppet has a lot of great movements and expressions.

So I turned this rabbit into a finger puppet with new legs, and he has become one of my favorite projects. If you strap a little guitar onto this rabbit and give him a crazy haircut, he can really rock!

### ✳ Cutting Fur

*When tracing patterns onto fur, determine which direction you want the fur to lie on the puppet. Then make sure all the pieces lie the same way. The secret to cutting pattern pieces out of fur is to make small snips with the tips of your scissors on the back of the fabric. This way you won't cut the edges of the shag on the other side.*

**TIP**

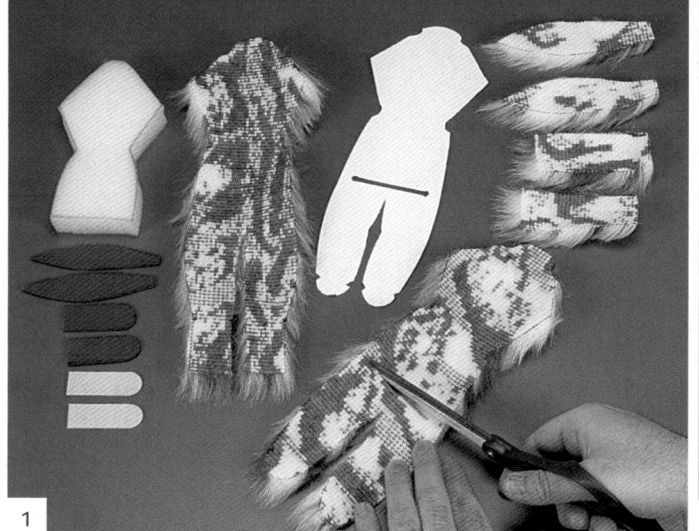

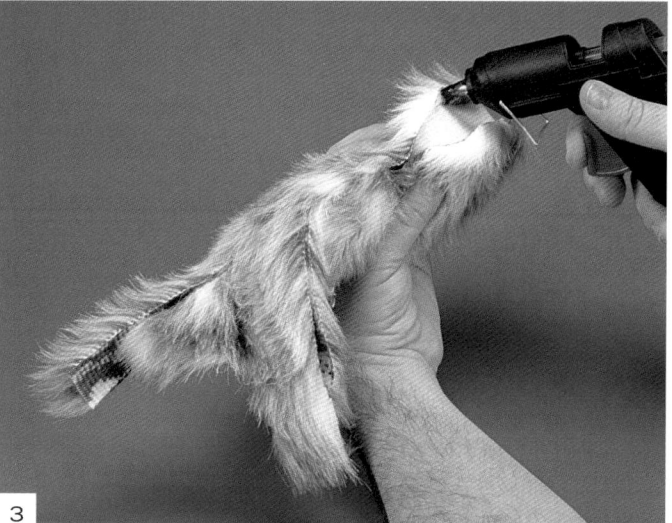

1 Trace and cut out all the patterns on page 51. You should have: one foam upper torso; one fur front body piece and one fur back body piece; two fur arms; two fur ears; two felt ears; two felt feet. Cut a craft stick into two pieces, each the same length as the foot pattern on page 51. 2 Center the foam torso between the two fur body pieces. Make sure it lines up so that the excess fur around the foam piece is even on all sides. Once everything is lined up, glue the foam torso to the inside the fur body pieces. 3 Put a line of glue on the edge of the fur around the foam torso, then press the fur edges together around the foam torso. Don't glue wherever there is a mark on the pattern, as this is where the arms and ears will attach. 4 Glue the leg pieces together next. Glue just along the edges of the fur. Make sure your fingers will fit in the openings of the legs. Glue the inseam first, making sure it is secure. Stop gluing at the marks at the ankle, making sure the marks match up on both the front and back fur body pieces.

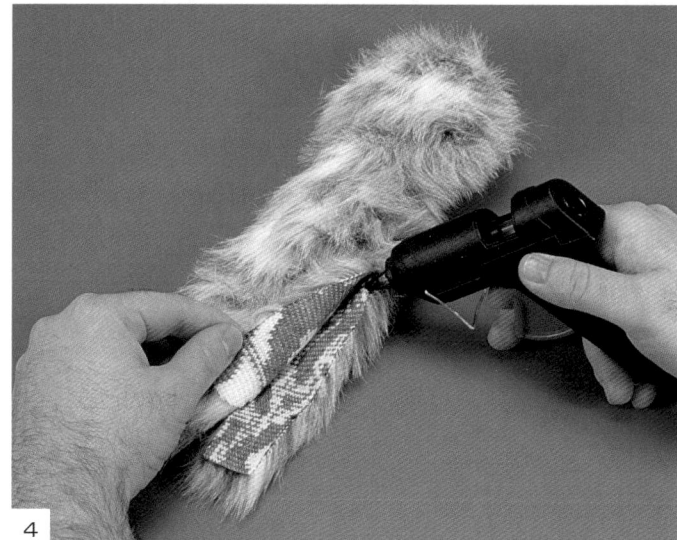

✳ *Pay attention to which way the fur is flowing. For the body, the fur should flow down, but for the ears, the fur should go up to a point. You can determine which way the fur flows when you arrange your patterns.*

TiP

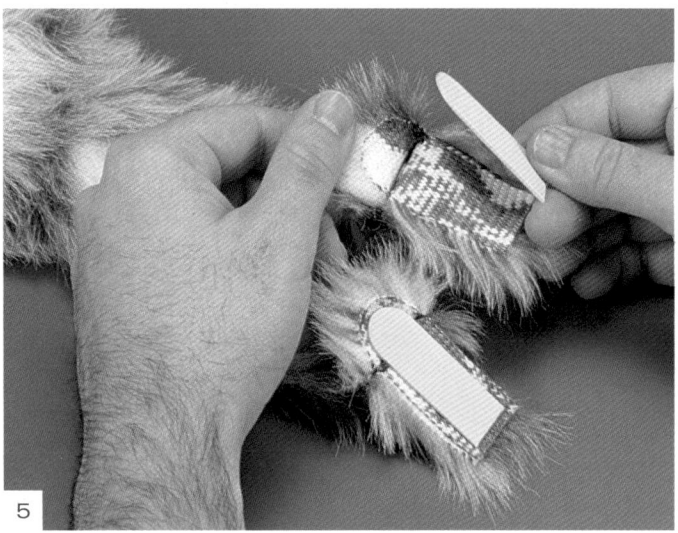

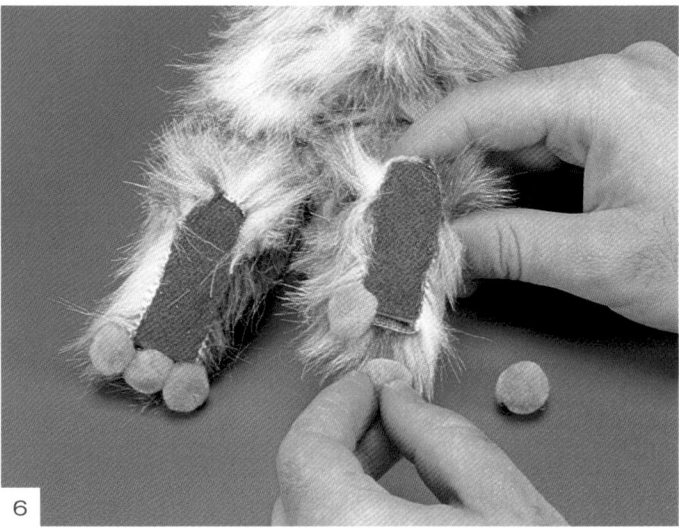

5

6

**5** Pull open the fur feet to the ankle marks. Glue a stick to the bottom of each foot, making sure the stick is held by both the front and back fur pieces. The round end of the stick is the heel, and the straight end will be where the toes go. **6** Glue the brown felt footpad on the craft stick. Add a line of glue around the edge of the felt and fold the excess fur over. Then add three ½" (13mm) tan pom-poms for the toes. Do this for both feet. **7** Take a fur arm and put a line of glue on the inside edge, then roll the arm closed. Do this for the other arm, trying to keep this seam as small as possible. Glue a ¾" (25mm) tan pom-pom on the side of each arm where the fur flows down. These will be the palms. Next, glue three ½" (13mm) tan pom-poms on the end of the arm as fingers, and another slightly offset as a thumb. **8** Glue the arms into the open spots you left in the body. If possible, glue the arm onto the foam torso. You might need to make a few minor gluing adjustments to make sure the seam is as clean as possible. Make sure the fur body is glued tightly around the arms.

7    8

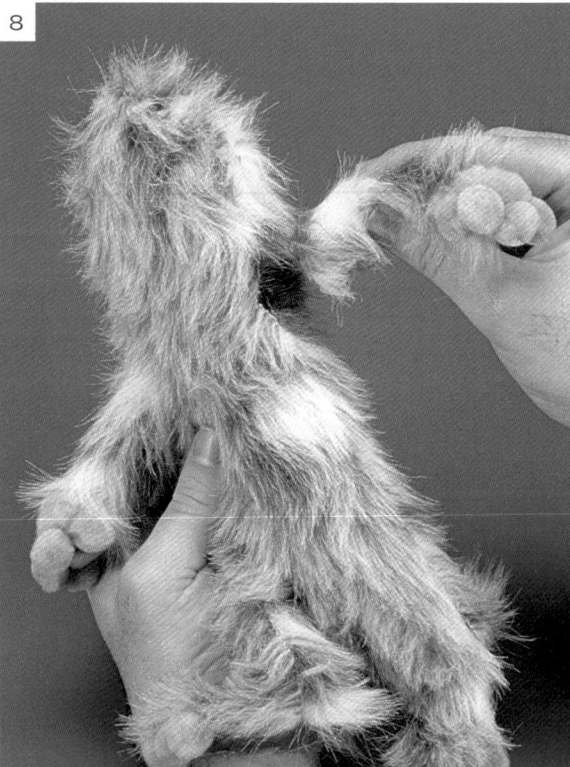

☆
## Puppeteering Secret #8

To add realism to Running Rabbit, cut the index and middle fingers off a black work glove. Wear the glove when you are performing with Running Rabbit. If possible, wear a long sleeved black shirt and perform before a black card or curtain. Your audience will focus more on the rabbit, and you will seem to disappear.

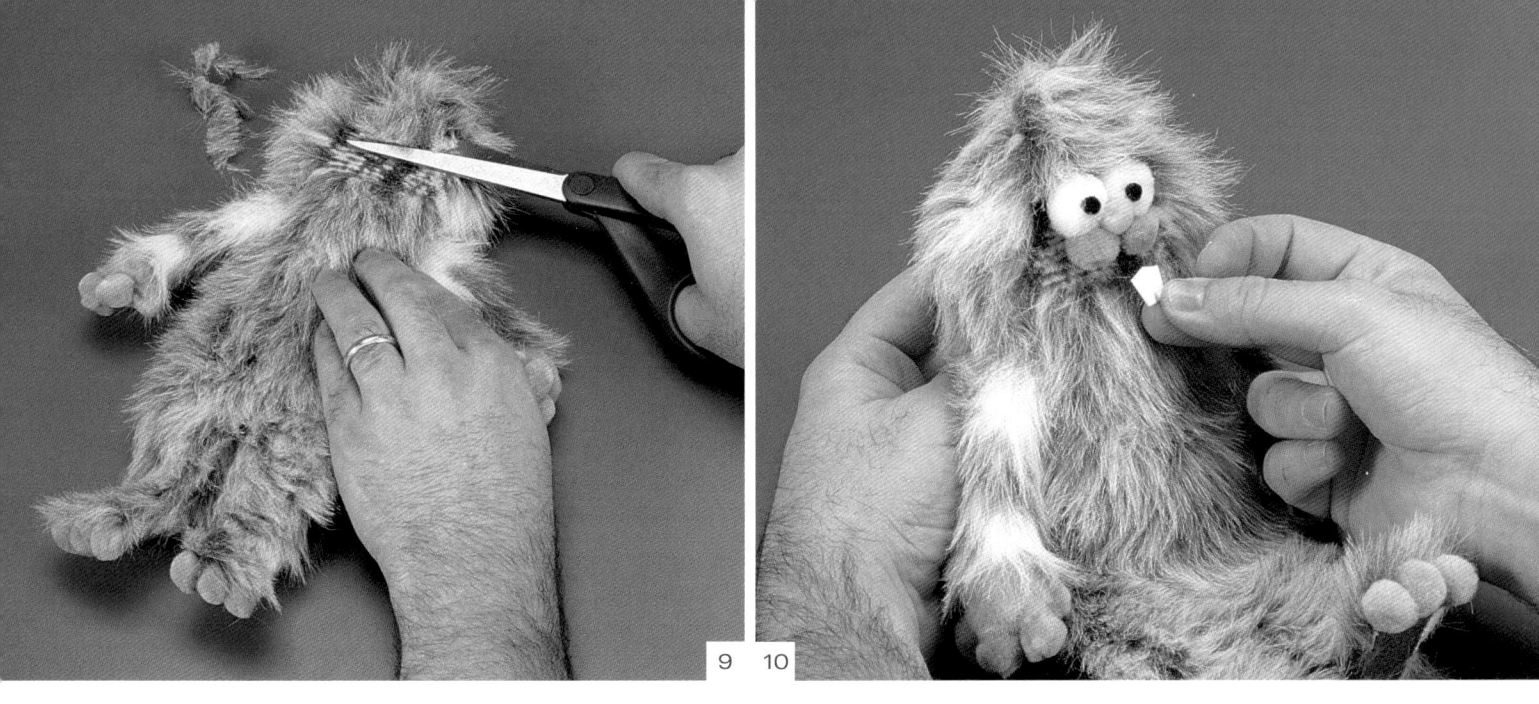

9 Use scissors to clip away the shaggy fur where the face will be. Brush the fur up before clipping, making sure not to cut too much. 10 Glue the eyes on the face, using ¾" (18mm) white pom-poms for the eyes, and two ³⁄₁₆" (5mm) black pom-poms for the pupils. Glue a ¼" (6mm) pink pom-pom below the eyes for the nose. Glue two ½" (13mm) tan pom-poms for cheeks below the nose. Finally, cut a small notch in the white sheet foam and smooth the teeth out before gluing them in place between the cheeks. You may want to trim the top of the teeth to fit perfectly between the cheeks. 11 Make the ears. Glue the brown felt ear on the fabric side of the shaggy fur ears. Then make a line of glue around the edge of the shaggy fur ear and around the edge of the brown felt, and roll the shaggy fur into the edge of the felt. This will make the ear seem more real. 12 Glue the ears to the head in the slots you left open on the head. If possible, glue the ears to the foam torso, and make sure the seams around the ear are as clean as possible.

TIP

✳ If you want the ears to really stand up, make a small cut into the foam torso piece and glue the ears into the foam and not just against it. If you want the ears to lie flat, just glue the ears to the fur body piece.

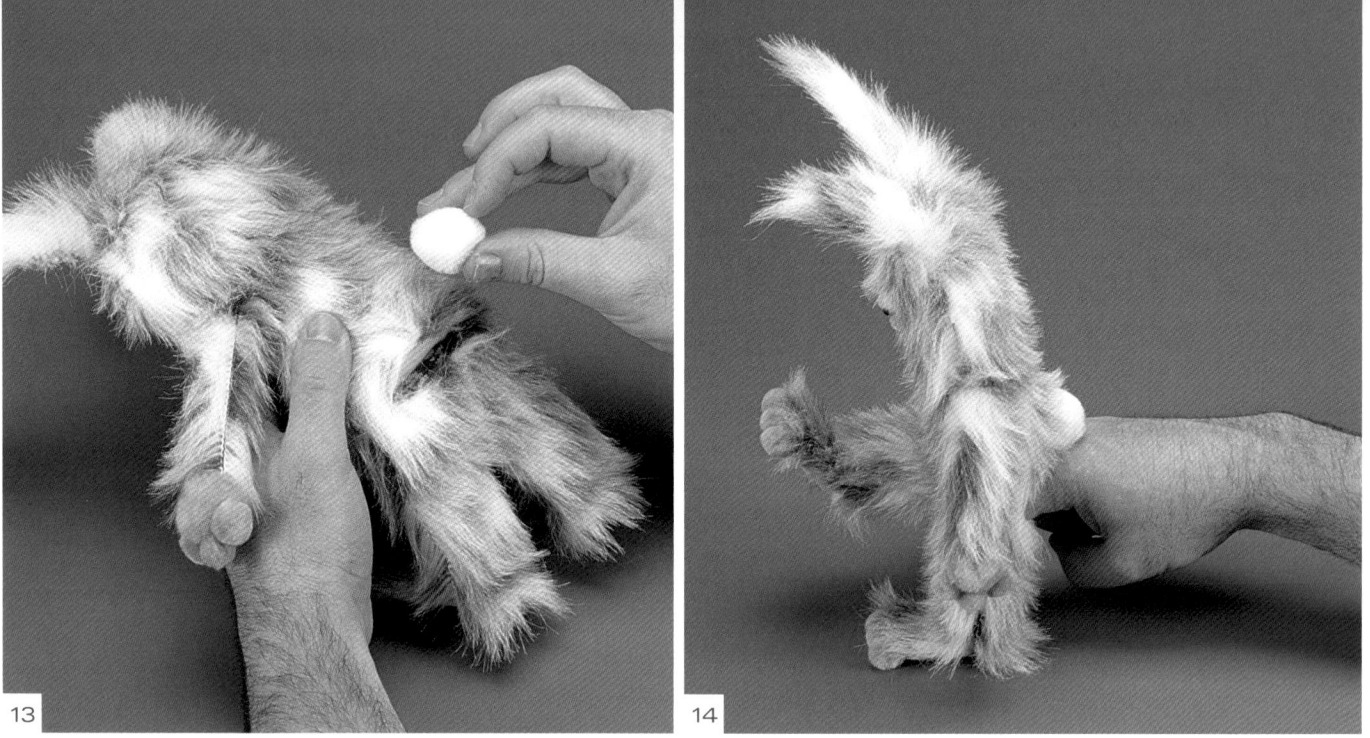

13

14

**13** Glue a 1″ (25mm) white pom-pom on the rabbit's back as a tail. The tail should be above where your fingers will go into the legs. Make sure the tail doesn't block your fingers. **14** Stick your index and middle finger into the legs.

## Make More Puppets!

Let's face it, the Running Rabbit is adorably cute. A simple change in fur color, or a slightly different face, will make a completely unique Running Rabbit. His size is perfect for little hats, clothes, tools and instruments. You can find these items in craft, hobby, and toy stores or in shops that supply dollhouse furniture.

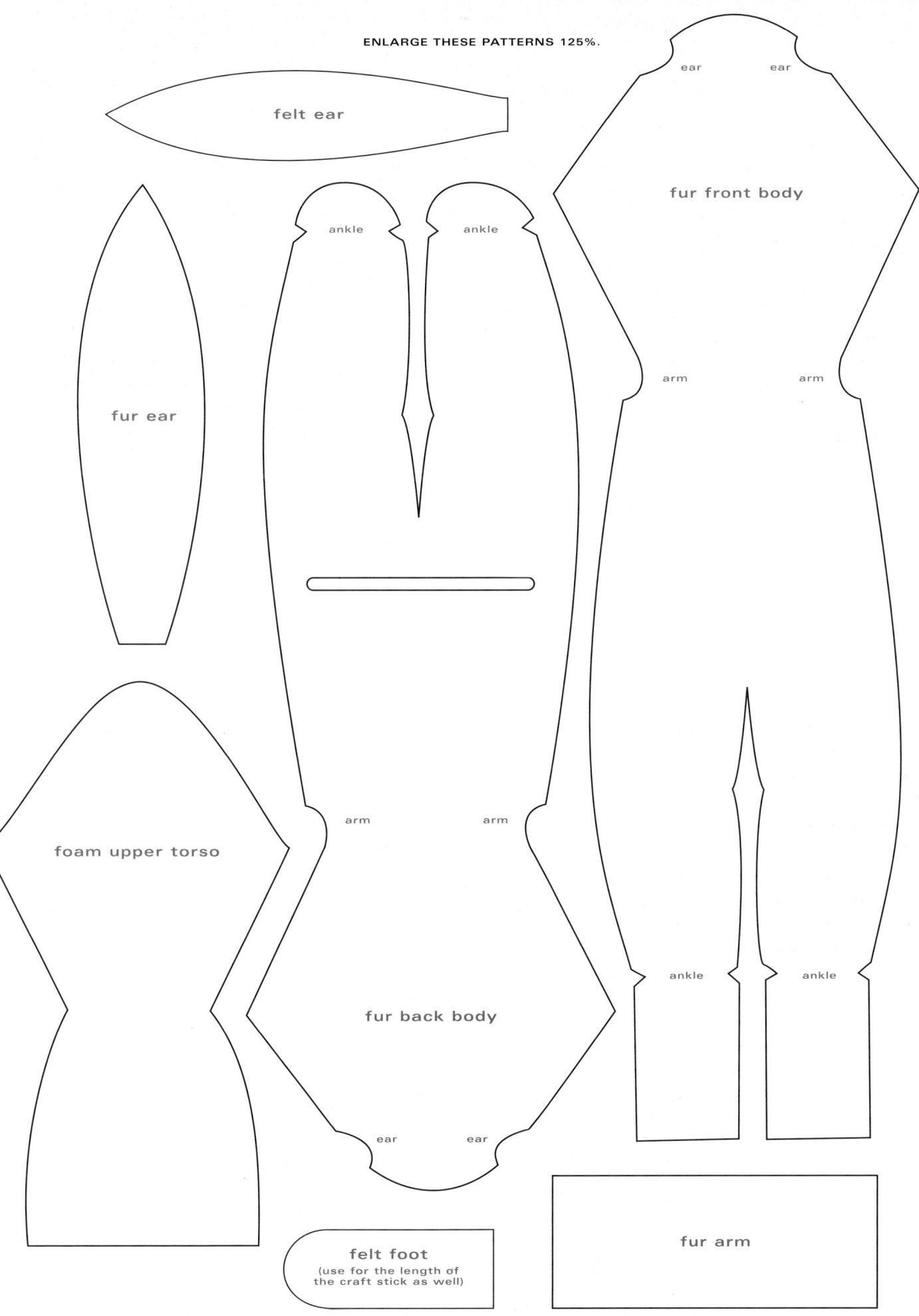

felt ear

fur front body

ear     ear

fur ear

ankle     ankle

arm     arm

foam upper torso

arm     arm

ankle     ankle

fur back body

ear     ear

felt foot
(use for the length of
the craft stick as well)

fur arm

**MATERIALS**

12" x 18" (30cm x 46cm)
piece of tan sheet foam

wooden spoon

wire coat hanger

three ½" (13mm) black pom poms

six ½" (13mm) tan pom poms

two 2" (5cm) green pom poms

pliers
*(with cutting edge)*

black permanent marker

scissors

glue gun

# BOXING KANGAROO

**puppet** *9* ▶

When I was nineteen, I had an agent who would book me to entertain at birthday parties and special events. Sometimes I would present a little show, but most of the time I did a strolling puppeteer act. I would walk around the party and use the puppet's arms to shake hands, give hugs, high five and joke around with the guests. As you can imagine, after four years I had quite a repertoire of arm rod moves and I still use them today.

The Boxing Kangaroo incorporates some punching moves that I fortunately never had to use at a party. Make up your own arm-rod moves. I had fun discovering mine. What moves will you discover for your Boxing Kangaroo?

✱ *You could paint the wooden spoon tan if you want, or use a different color of sheet foam to make a variety of kangaroos.*

**T*I*P**

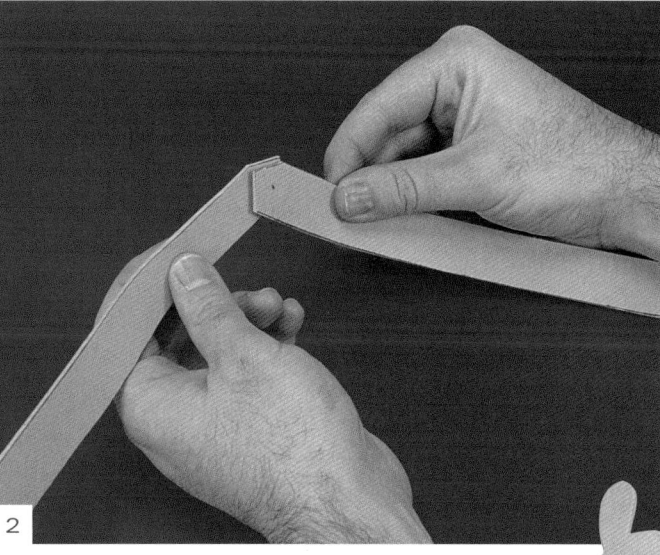

**1** Trace and cut out all the patterns on page 55 from the tan sheet foam. **2** Glue the ends of the two arms together. Match up the marks on the end of the arm before gluing. The marks should create a bend in the arm. **3** Carefully thread the glued arms through the two arm slots in the foam body of the kangaroo. **4** Glue the neck of the kangaroo body around the spoon by wrapping the body, and not just the arms, around the spoon. Glue the foam body securely to the spoon as well. Then glue the sides of the tail and the back seam together. The foam body should now be attached to the spoon. To make the kangaroo more secure, glue the back to the spoon, as well. **5** With pliers, cut the hook from a wire coat hanger.

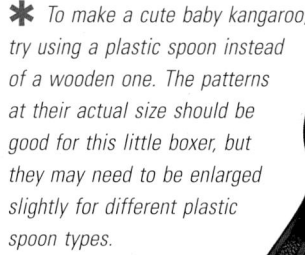

## BABY KANGAROO

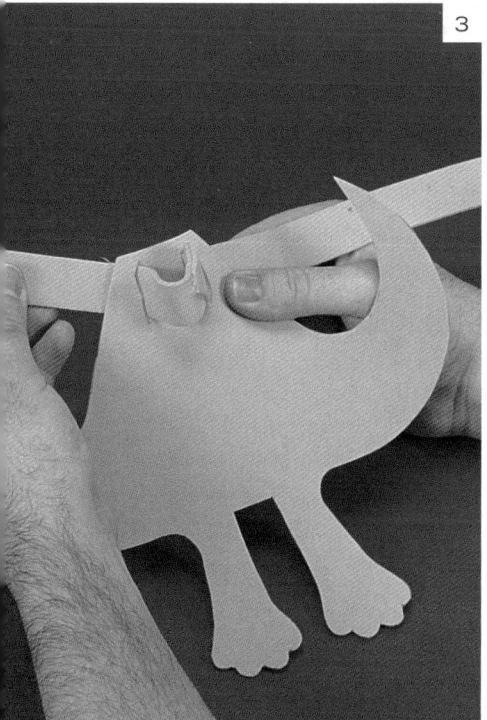

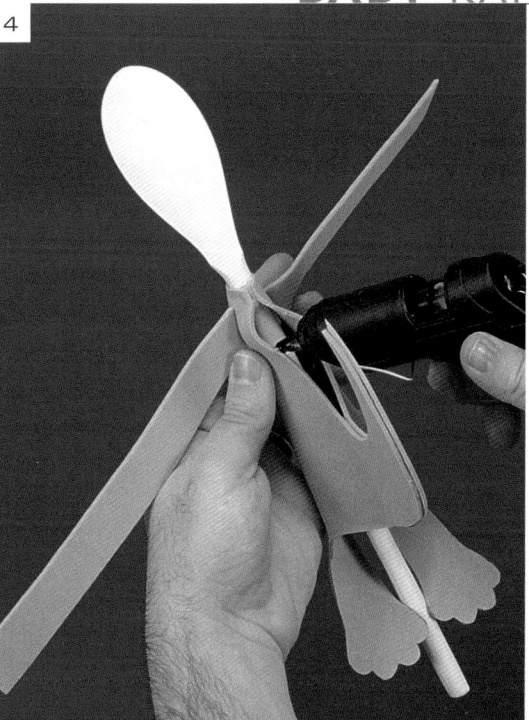

✻ *To make a cute baby kangaroo, try using a plastic spoon instead of a wooden one. The patterns at their actual size should be good for this little boxer, but they may need to be enlarged slightly for different plastic spoon types.*

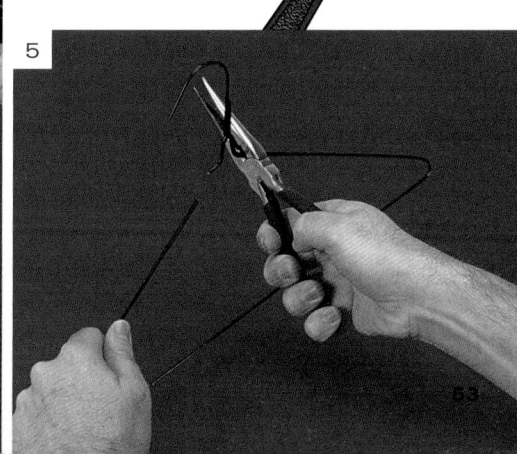

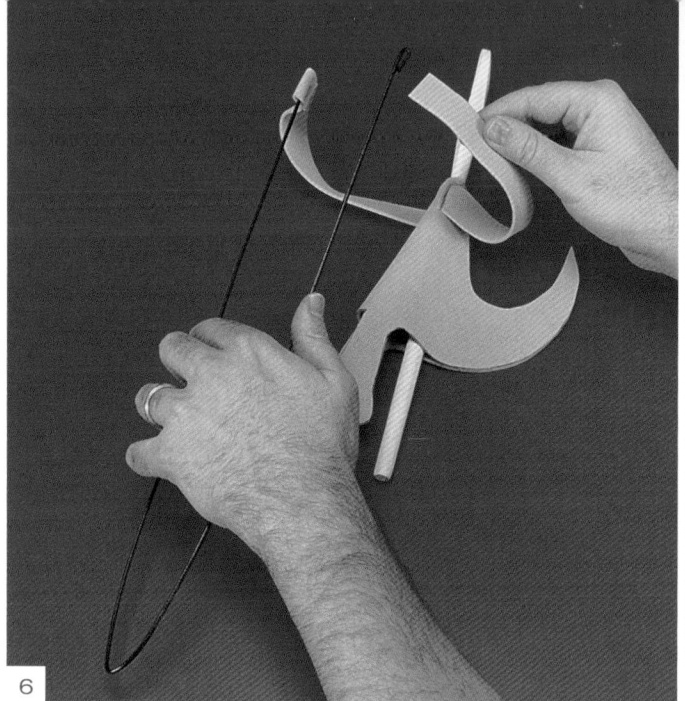
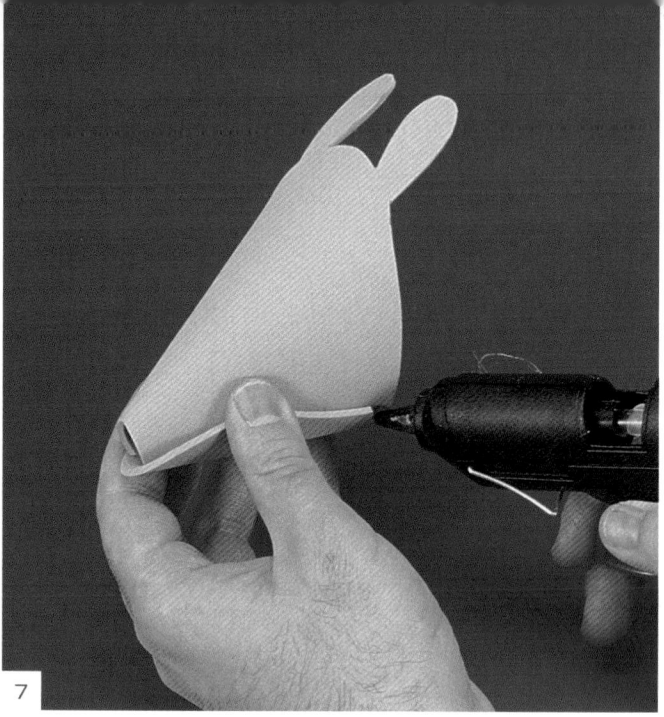

**6** Carefully straighten out the coat hanger, and then bend it in half, making a V shape. Bend down the tips of the wire for safety, making sure there are no sharp points. Finally, wrap the hands of the kangaroo around the bent ends of the wire and glue them securely in place. **7** Glue the head and chin together. The chin holds the two edges of the head together.

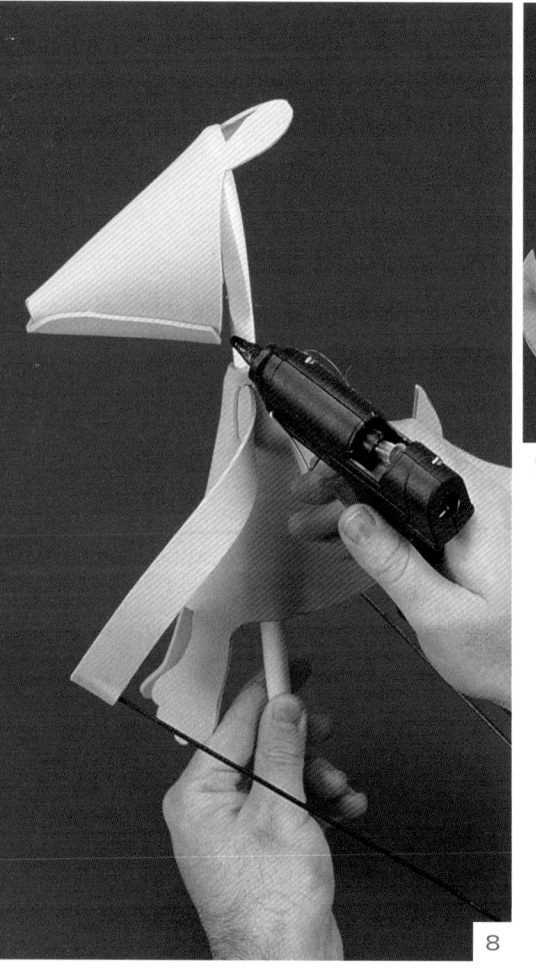
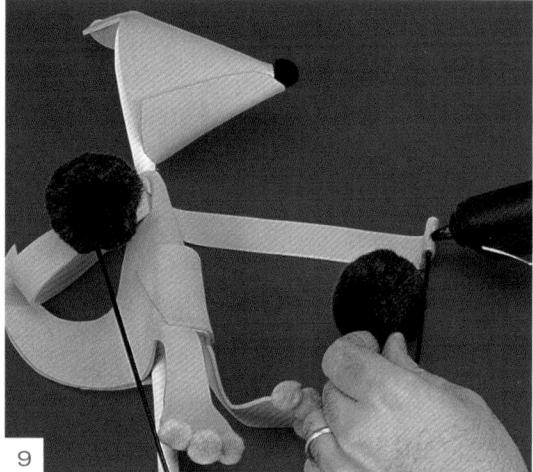
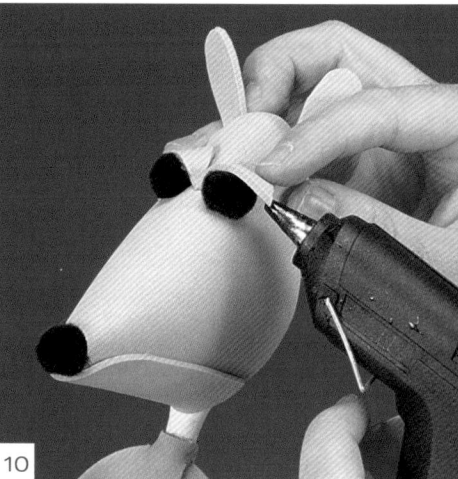

**8** Glue the head onto the top of the spoon: Glue the edge of the spoon, and then place the head on the edge you glued. The head of the kangaroo should touch the top of the spoon, and the neck should touch the handle. **9** Glue on a black pom-pom for the nose. Glue three tan pom-poms on each foot for his toes. The pom-poms on the feet are more secure if you glue in between the toe marks on the pattern. Bend the feet forward. Glue the optional pouch to the center of the kangaroo's body. Glue the large green pom-poms on the hands for boxing gloves. **10** Bend the ears forward. Next, glue the black pom-pom eyes on the head, and then glue the eyelids over the eyes. You may need to trim the eyelids a little to make them look neat.

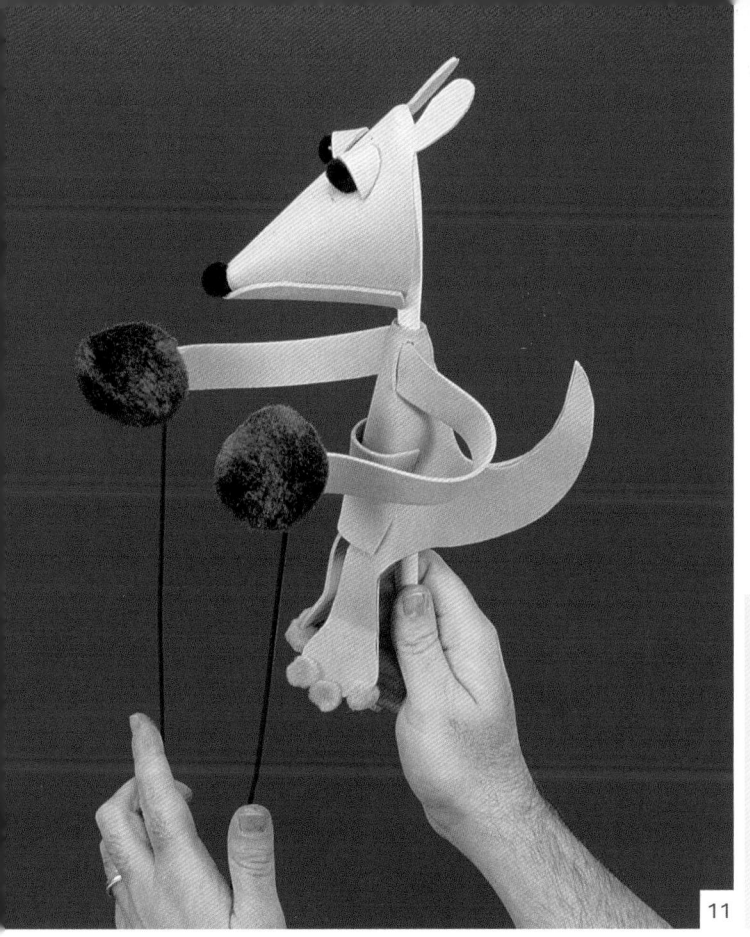

**11** Hold the spoon in one hand and work the coat hanger rods with the other.

☆
## Puppeteering Secret #9

Need some help performing with Boxing Kangaroo? See page 15 for some great boxing moves! Try putting something in the pouch to give the audience a clue about Boxing Kangaroo's personality.

**ENLARGE THESE PATTERNS 200%.**

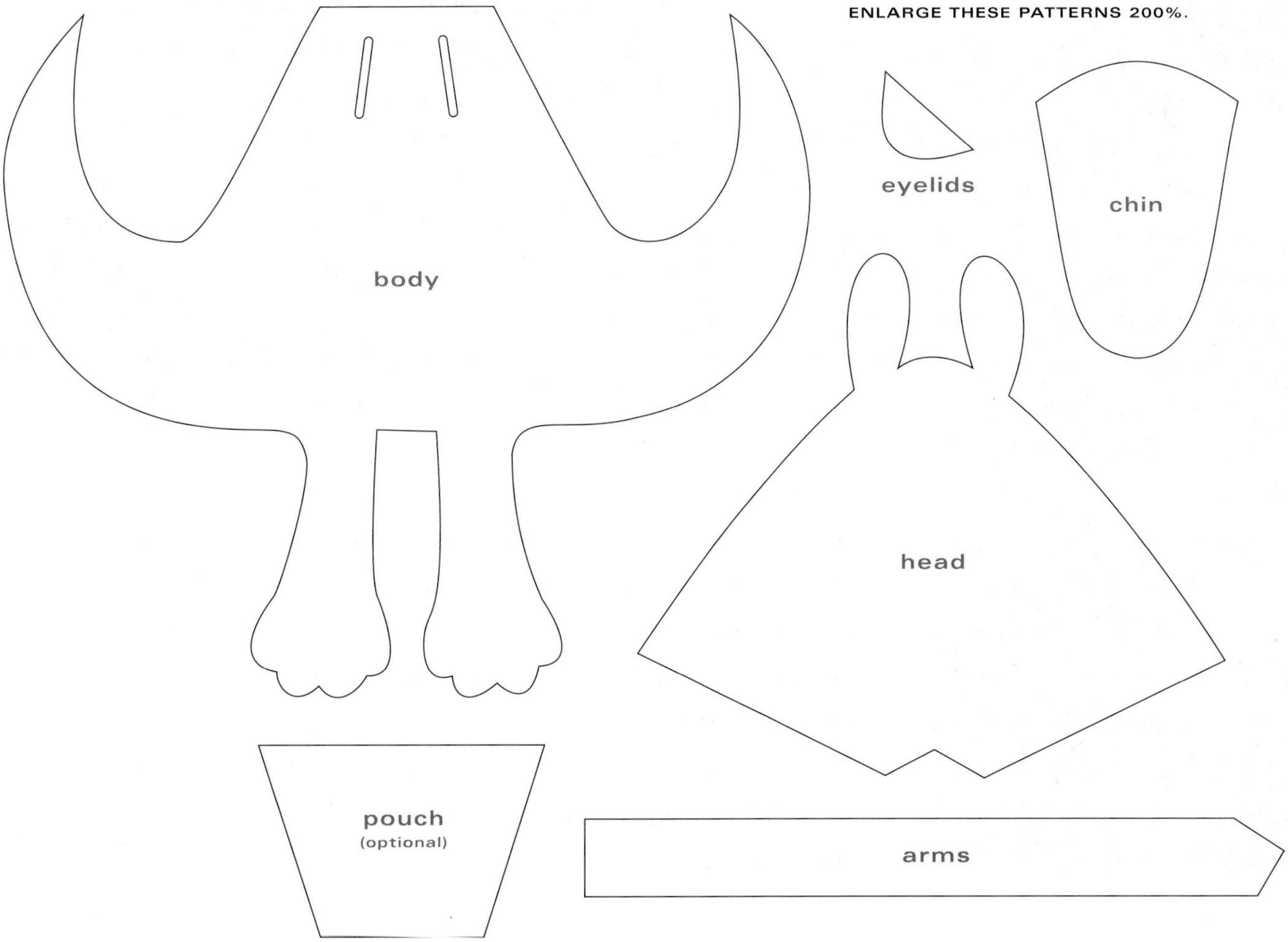

body

eyelids

chin

head

pouch
(optional)

arms

MATERIALS

two 3" (8cm) squares of brown felt

5" (13cm) square of red felt

two 10" (25cm) squares of fur

two heavy 9" (23cm) paper plates

walnut shell

craft stick

one 1" (25mm) black pom-pom

permanent marker

pen or pencil

scissors

glue gun

# NUTTY BEAR

puppet 10 ▶

My first job on a prime-time sitcom was moving eyelids, much like the ones on Nutty Bear. After I finished working at Disney World I went to Los Angeles for a two-week audition for a new TV show called *Dinosaurs*. A lot of puppeteers auditioned, but I was one of four who made it. The job I got was moving the eyes of Baby Sinclair. I was twenty-three, working in Hollywood, and doing a job that I had started rehearsing for when I was eight.

The thing I learned about moving eyes is that the little moves are just as important as the big ones. As always, practice makes perfect.

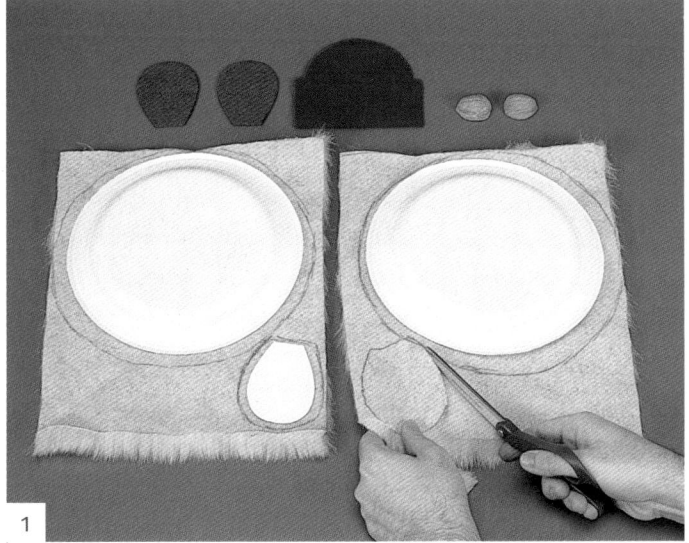

1

2

✳ *Walnuts have a natural mark at the halfway point of their shells. Just split your walnut along that mark.*

TiP

**1** Trace the patterns on page 61 and cut out the ears from the brown felt and the mouth from the red felt. Then trace and cut out the ears using the fur. The fur ears should be a little larger than the felt ears, so cut an extra ½" (13mm) of fur around each ear. Then trace and cut out, using the plates as the pattern, the two head pieces from the fur. Leave an extra ½" (13mm) of fur around each plate. Finally, split your walnut shell into two equal pieces. **2** To make the face, use the pattern to trace the mouth on the back of a plate. Then position the walnut halves where the eyes will be and trace around the shells. Try to line up the side points of the shells horizontally as you trace them onto the plate. **3** Use a permanent marker to color inside the eyes on the plate, making pupils for the bear. You can make the irises any color you wish. **4** Cut around the top half of each eye, stopping the cut at the halfway mark of the eye, then cut outside the same line so you can remove a thick, U-shaped piece around each eye. Fold the eyes down in half along the cut. Make a similar double cut below the mouth. Make sure the double cut for the mouth is not too wide; otherwise the felt will not cover it.

3

4

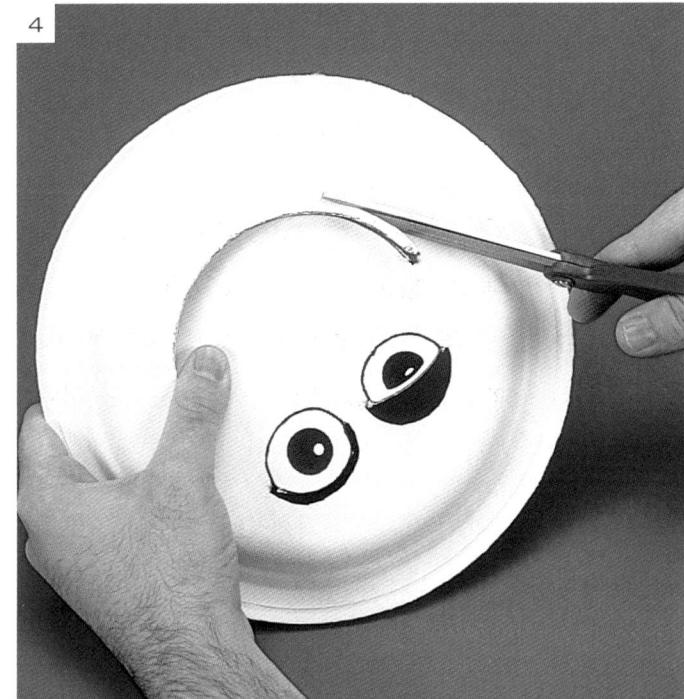

5

6

**5** Using the face plate as a pattern, trace the eyes and mouth onto the back of one of the fur head pieces. Make sure you consider the direction of the fur before cutting. Remove the plate and finish drawing the shell-shaped eyes on the back of the fur. Cut out the eyes on the fur face, and then cut out the line of the mouth. **6** Glue the nutshells onto the folded half of the eyes on the inside of the plate. The shells will extend beyond the part of the eye that folds and into the inside of the plate. Make sure you use a good amount of glue on the shells. **7** Glue the craft stick on the unglued half of the shells. Put glue on the shells, then slide the stick under them and hold it in place. This will let you control Nutty Bear's blinking. **8** Place a single line of glue along the top edge of the smile slot inside the plate. Then press the edge of the mouth felt just on the line of glue. Make sure the smile line of the felt and the cut in the plate match up. The line of glue and the edge of the mouth felt should also line up.

7  8

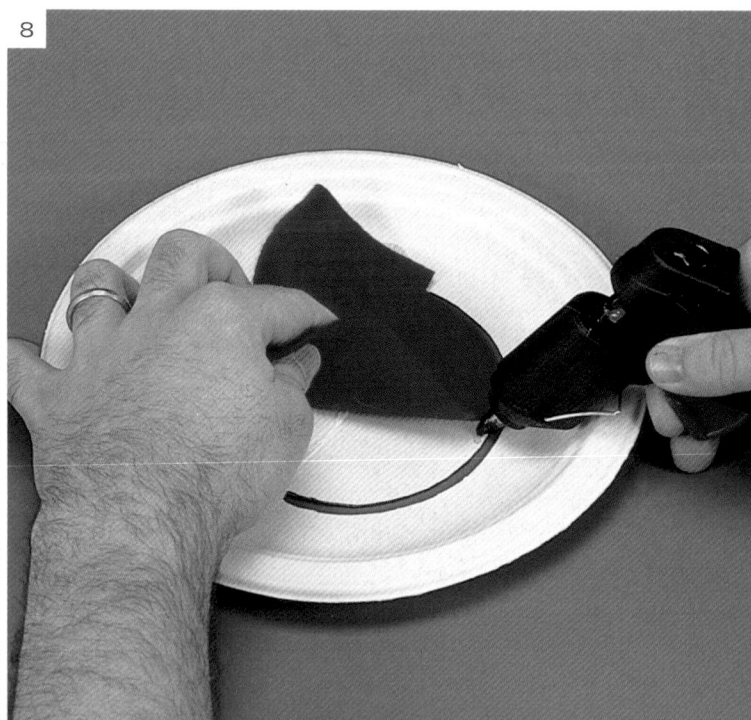

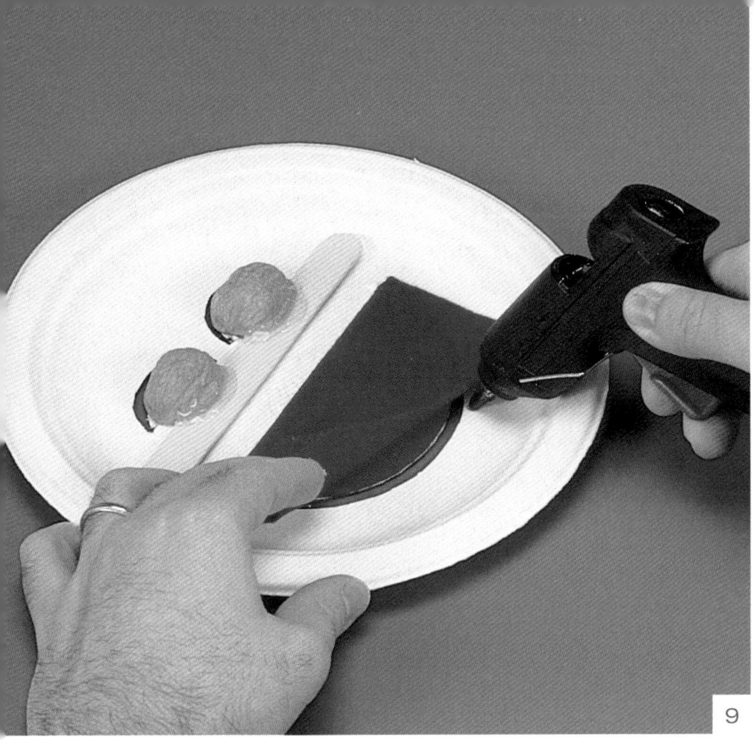

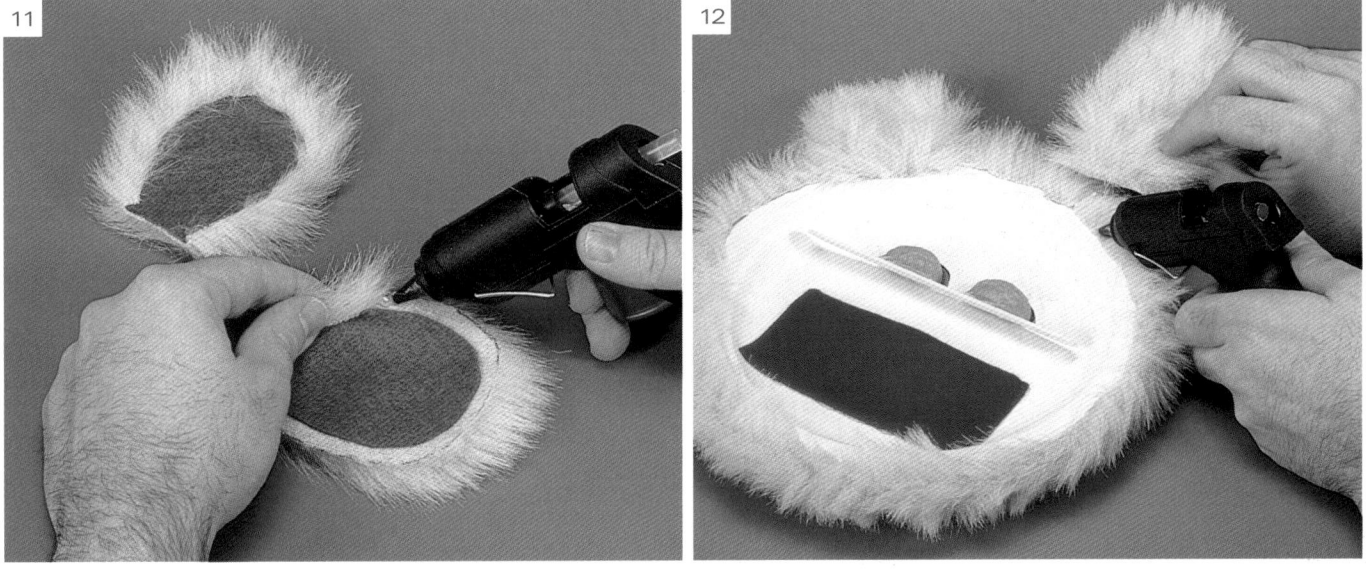

**9** Place a single line of glue on the bottom of the smile slot. Fold over the rest of the felt and press it against the glue. **10** Glue the head fur to the outside of both plates. Set the plate in the center of the fur, and roll and glue the edges of the fur over the edge of the plate. For the front of the face, line up the eyes and mouth before gluing. Make sure you have glue in the center of the face, around the eyes and mouth. Glue the fur firmly to the plate. **11** Glue the felt ears inside the fur ears. Glue the felt down, and then roll the edges of the fur onto the felt. **12** Glue the ears on the face plate. Make sure the ears are secure.

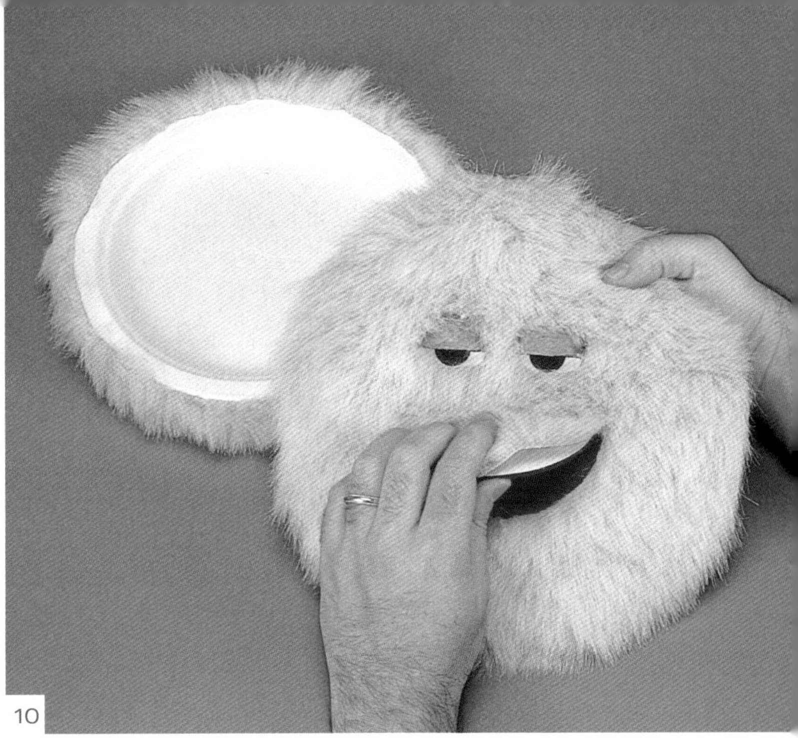

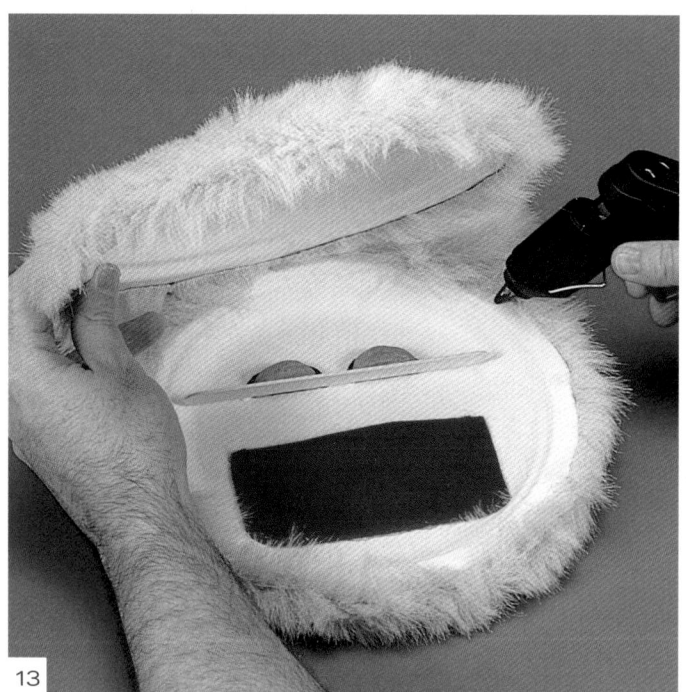

13

14

**13** Glue the face and back head plates together. Glue only the top half of the plates together, leaving the bottom open for your hands to use the puppet. **14** Glue the black pom-pom on the face for the nose. **15** Position your hand inside the mouth, and use your index finger to operate the eyes. For this picture we removed the back of Nutty Bear so you could see the hand position.

## NUTTY BEAR **JOBS**

15

✱ *The Nutty Bear is a great puppet for teachers. He might signal nap time at a preschool or play hide-and-seek with the kids. He might also need students to wake him up to tell a story or share some news. His eye-closing gag could become a daily ritual for the kids.*

**Blinking Nutty Bear** To make Nutty Bear a little more clever, you can make him wink by cutting the craft stick in half so the eyes blink independantly. You may have to use more than one finger with this variation. If you find it too difficult, try creating only one eye that moves first. That way, you can make a practice bear. To do this, follow the same directions, but when you come to cutting out the eyes, only cut out the eye you want to blink.

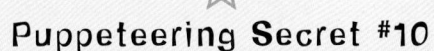

**Puppeteering Secret #10**

Need some help performing with Nutty Bear? Go back to page 13 for some tips on using Nutty Bear in a show.

THESE PATTERNS APPEAR AT FULL SIZE.

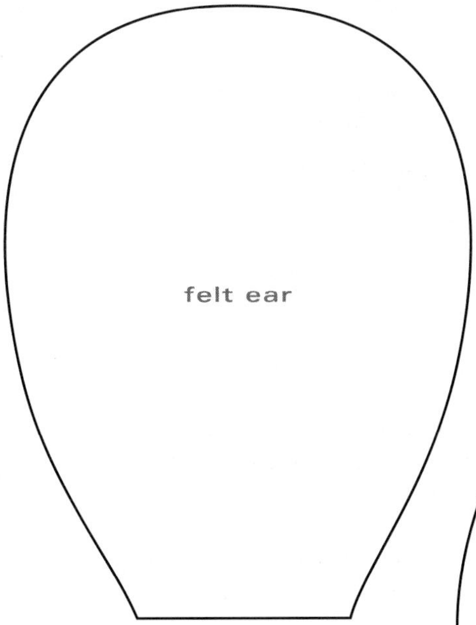

felt ear

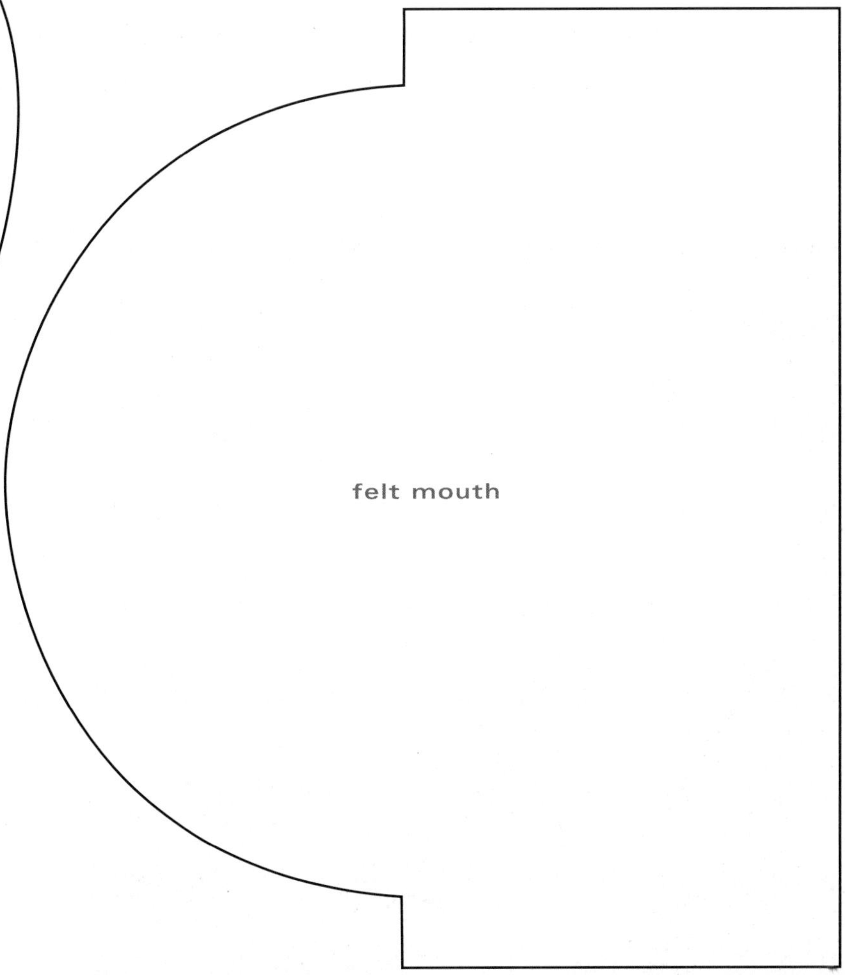

felt mouth

MATERIALS

12" (30cm) square
of tan short shag fur

5" (13cm) square of
1" (3cm) foam rubber

1" x 10" (3cm x 25cm)
strip of 1" (3cm) foam

two 20 oz. paper bowls

7" (18cm) square of black felt

1" x 10" (3cm x 25cm) strip of felt

7" (18cm) paper plate

20" x 10" (51cm x 25cm)
piece of purple short shag fur

12" (30cm) square of
purple short shag fur *(for head)*

4" (10cm) diameter piece
of white long shag fur *(for hair)*

pom-poms *(optional facial features)*

pencil

black permanent marker

scissors

glue gun

double-sided tape *(optional)*

# BOWL OF A
# THOUSAND FACES

*puppet* **11** ▶ When I was younger, I used to sell the puppets I made. I made everything from latex puppets that looked like company CEOs to radio-controlled Santa costumes that had moving facial features. Once, an elementary school had me make them a set of puppets with hook and loop fasteners. You could make new puppet characters by using the fasteners to change the eyes, noses and wigs on the puppets. I liked those puppets, but I like the Bowl of a Thousand Faces better because you can use a lot of intricate facial details to make completely different puppets, and all you have to do is switch the bowls. The bowls pop into place so you can change faces in a flash. Once you create this puppet, a thousand faces are waiting to be made.

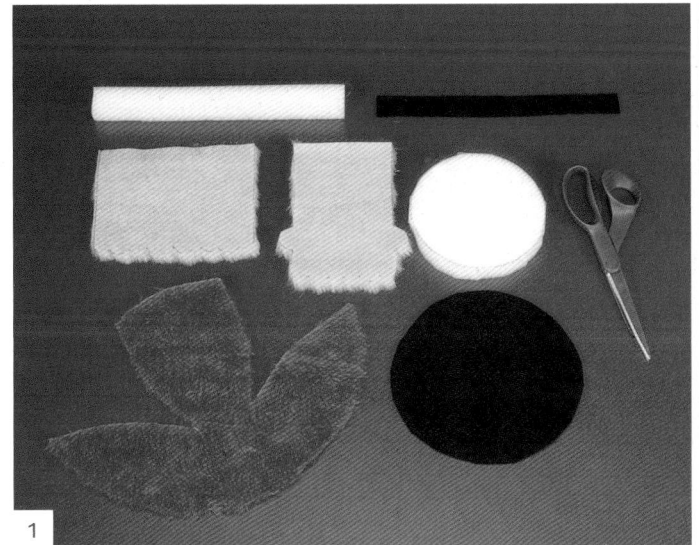

**1** Trace and cut out the following patterns from page 67: the purple short shag head, two short shag hands and two short shag feet. Cut one foam circle (5" [13cm] across), one large foam strip (10" [25cm] long), one felt strip 10" (25cm) long and one felt circle (the size of your plate) as well. **2** Glue the circle of black felt inside the plate and the circle of foam inside one of the bowls. **3** Fold the plate in half and glue half of the plate on the rim of the bowl. Glue the foam strip on the other half of the rim of the bowl. **4** To make the body, glue the 10" (25cm) felt strip to the shorter edge of a 20" x l0" (51cm x 25cm) purple short shag fur piece. Lay the felt on the very edge of the fur piece, and glue only half the felt strip to the fur, leaving half hanging over the end.

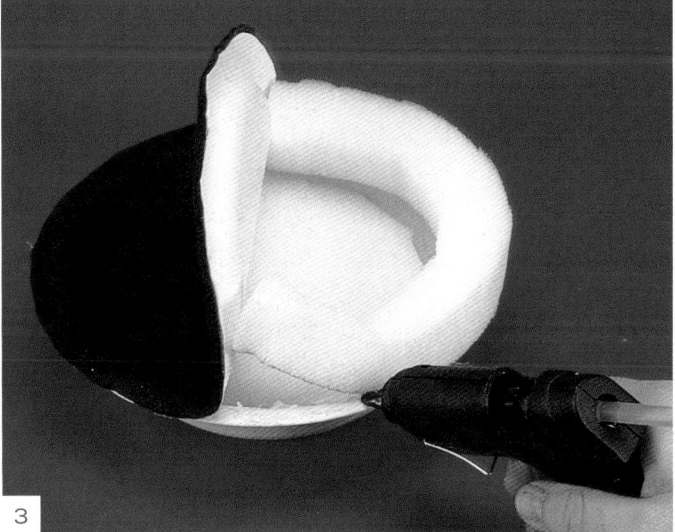

✳ *If you want, you can sew the body together, rather than using a felt strip to glue the body together.*

TIP

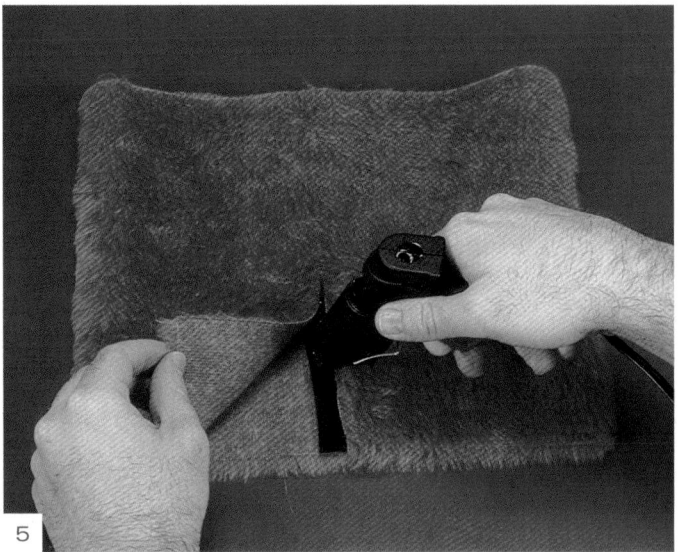

5

6

✳ *If you want to spice up your Bowl of a Thousand Faces you can use pom-poms for the toes. Just glue a 1" (25mm) pom-pom for each big toe, and a ½" (13mm) pom-pom for the other toes. You can even cut little felt toenails if you want to get really fancy.*

TIP

**5** Fold the ends of the shag fur body together, and glue the unattached end of the shag fur to the unattached edge of the felt strip. You should now have a closed loop of short shag fur. **6** To the hands, put a line of glue on only one edge of a hand, then fold the hand in half and smooth, keeping the edges as close as possible to hide the seam. Do this for the other hand. Glue and fold the feet, but glue all sides closed. **7** Glue the edge of the shag body to the foam strip on the bowl with the felt strip in the back of the puppet. The bowl should be above the shag body. Glue only on the foam strip and not on the bowl, so only half of the shag body is attached to the bowl. **8** Glue the other side of the shag body to the bottom half of the folded plate. Only the felt-covered surface of the plate should be showing. The fur should be glued over the lip of the plate.

7    8

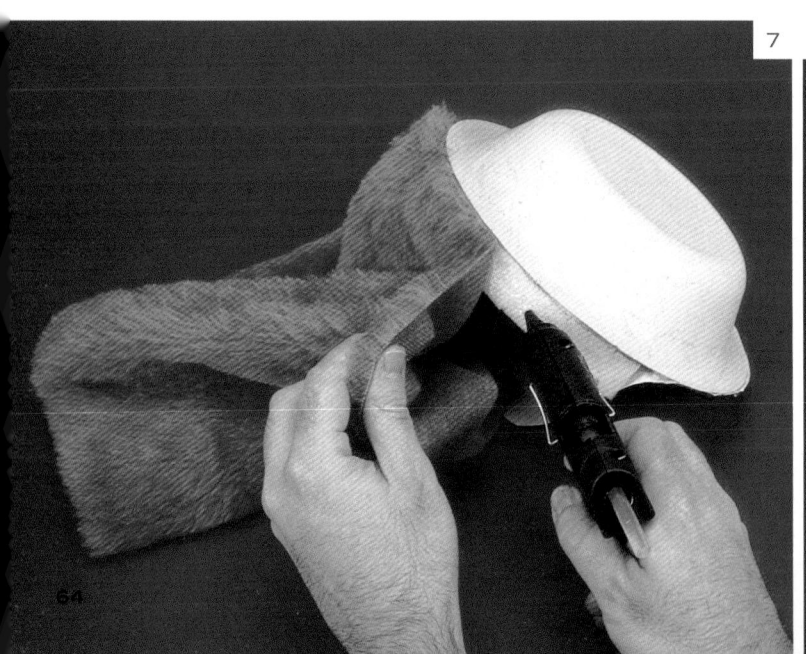

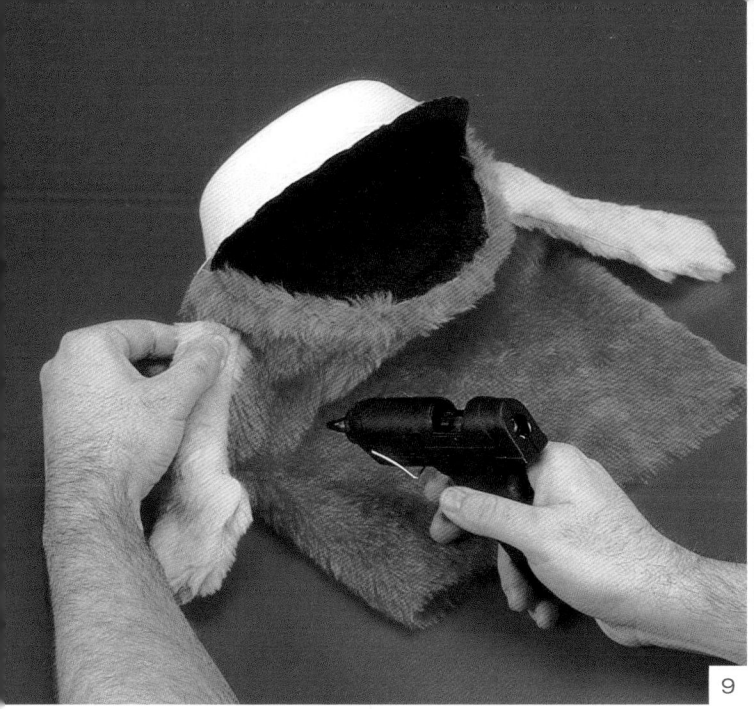 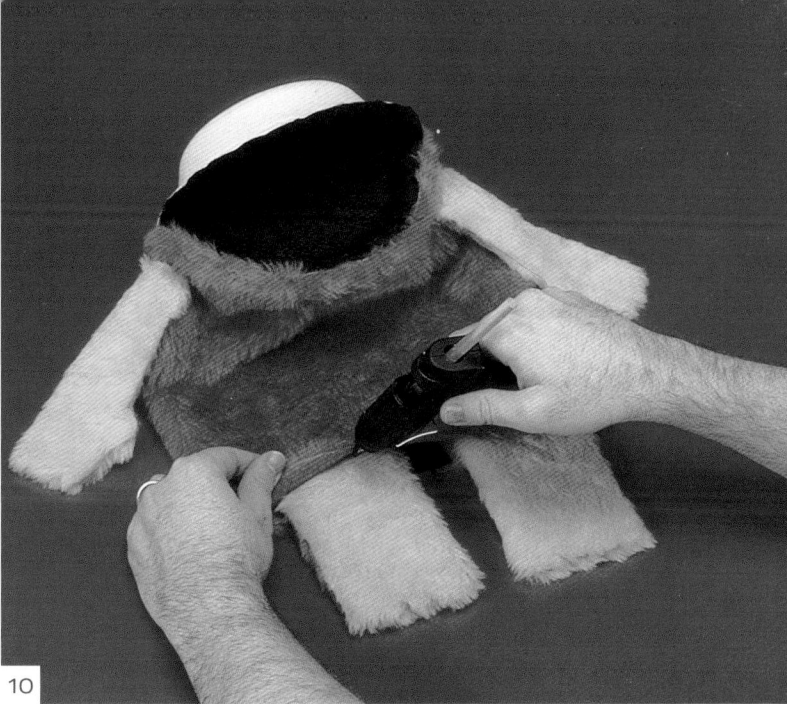

9   10

**9** Glue the hands on the short shag fur body of the puppet. The hands should attach to either side of the puppet, about 1" (3cm) below the edge of the plate. **10** Glue the feet on the bottom of the puppet, inside the front of the puppet. Leave a 2" (5cm) gap between the feet, and make sure that the big toes are on the inside of the feet. **11** Put a spot of glue on the front of each foot about 1½" (4cm) above the toes and fold the foot up. This will create a bend in the foot and give the leg some dimension. **12** Glue the shag fur head to the bowl. Bring the edges of the fur together and glue the seams. Do not roll the fur under the rim of the bowl. When the two bowls fit together you want nothing between them.

TIP

✱ *Depending on the size and depth of your bowls, you may have to make some pattern adjustments. The entire bowl should be covered, and the fur should hang a little over the lip of the bowl.*

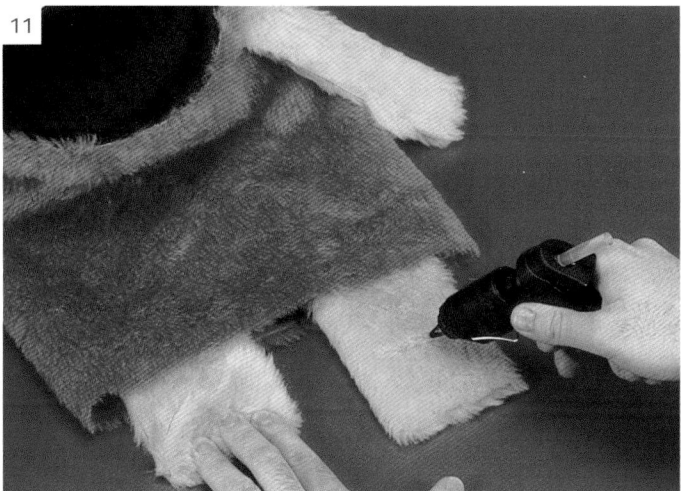

11

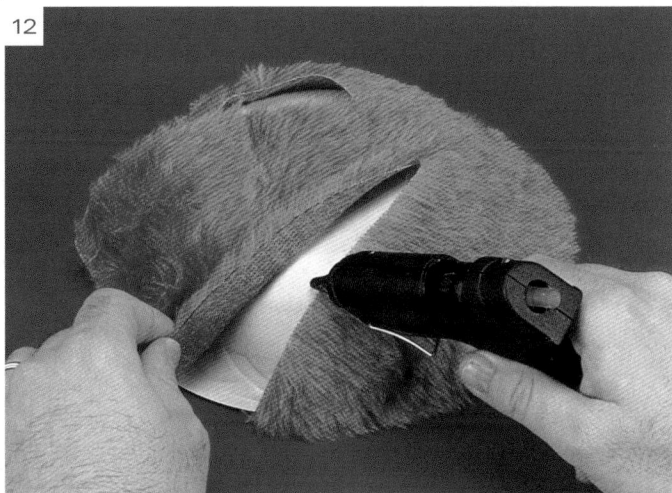

12

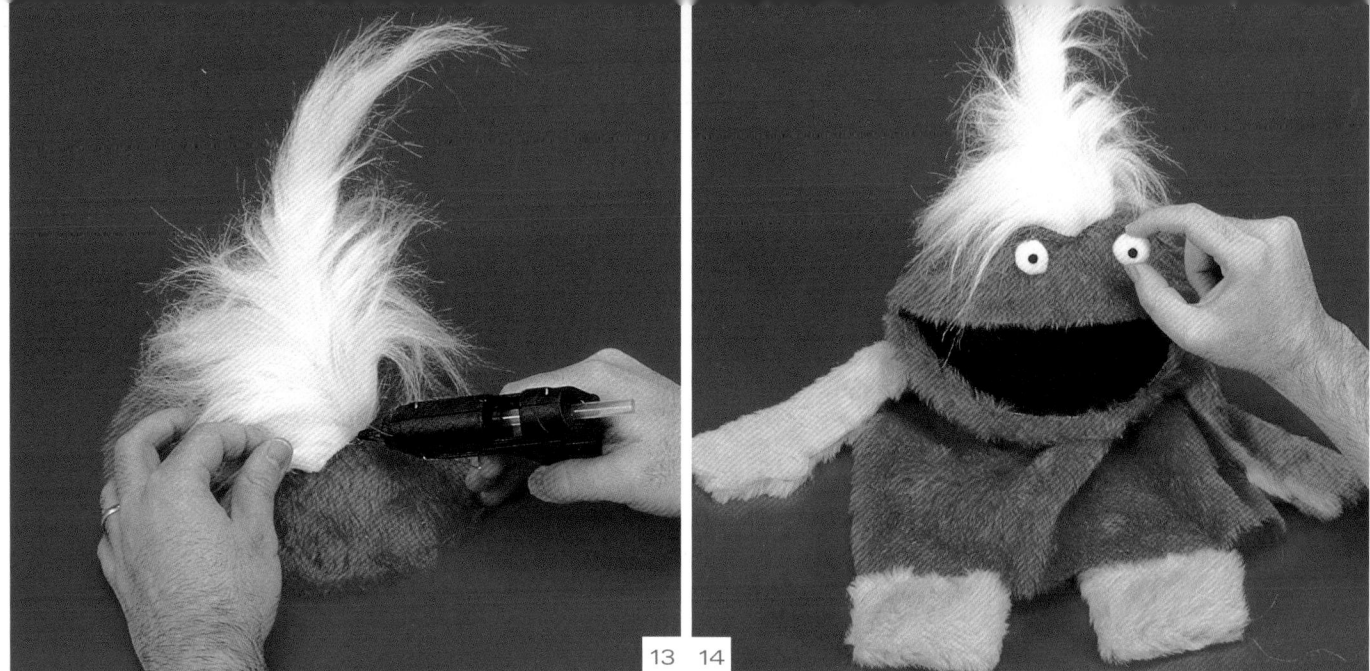

**13** Cut a patch of shaggy fur and glue it onto the head of your puppet. This will be the puppet's hair. Bunch the hair up and style it as you want. **14** Add eyes and a nose to your puppet head. Use pom-poms and other decorations to design the face you want. **15** Attach the face bowl of the puppet to the body of the puppet. Use double-stick tape, if you want, to attach the bowls. Stick your hand in the bottom of the puppet and use your hand to move the mouth.

**Make More Puppets!** For a challenge, try making enough different faces to do an entire production with one puppet. Each time a new character appears in the script, just switch faces. Kids love to watch puppet shows like this, because they can see the "magic" of the show. At the end, they would love to have a "Bowl of a Thousand Faces" of their own.

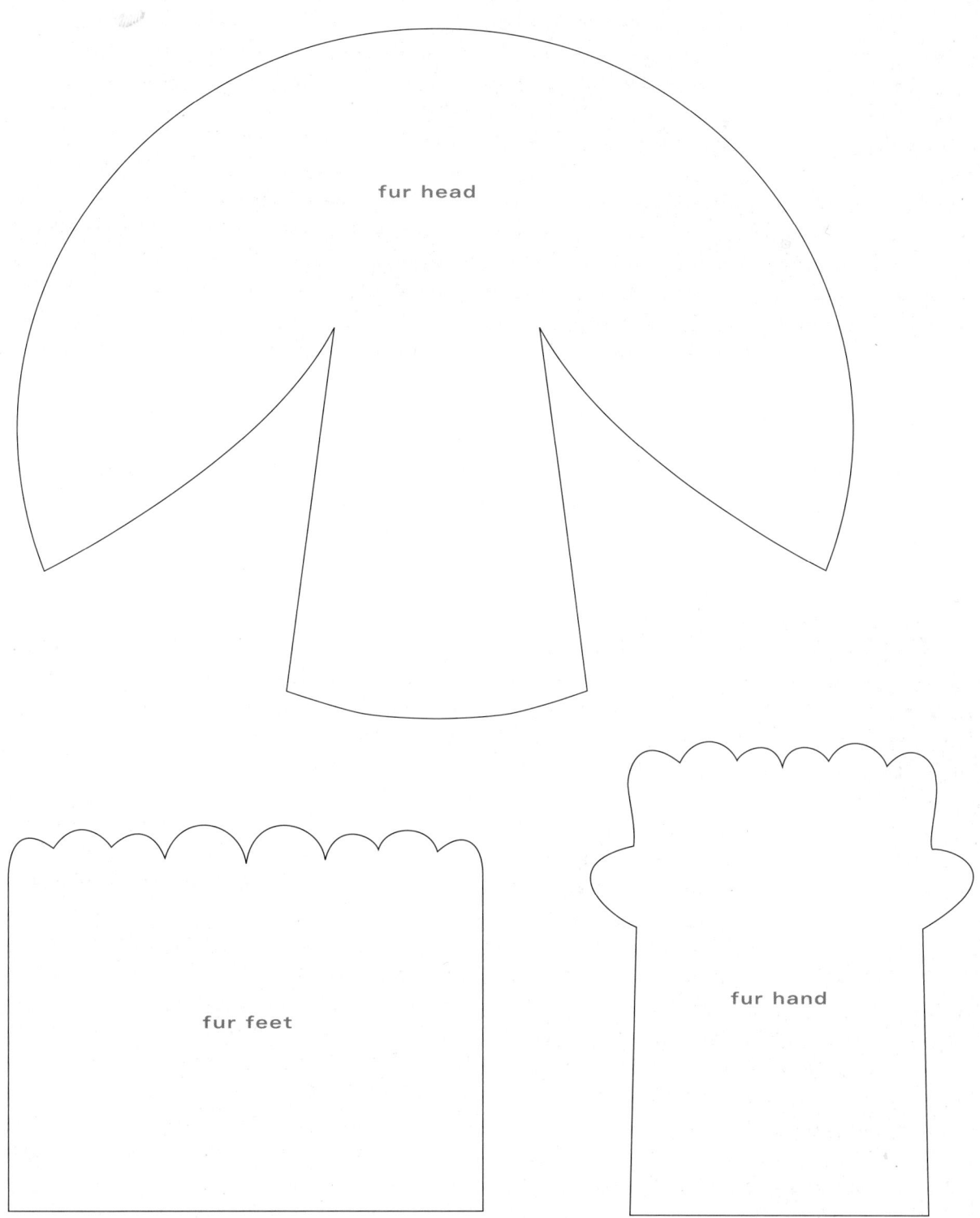

fur head

fur feet

fur hand

**ENLARGE THESE PATTERNS TO 200%.**

## MATERIALS

one wooden spoon

two blocks of white polymer clay

one block of red polymer clay

one block of blue polymer clay

one block of black polymer clay

one block of yellow polymer clay

one block of orange polymer clay

6" (15cm) of elastic cord

1' (30cm) of string
(dental floss or fishing line will work)

small metal or plastic ring

toothpicks

baking sheet

aluminum foil

oven

# SPOON CHICKEN

**puppet 12 ▶**

One summer when I was working in New York, I noticed a new craft store opening up across the street from my apartment. It had a crafters area in the back for artists to teach classes, so I asked if I could teach there. They were interested in seeing what I would build, so I put a spoon puppet workshop together. I never could free up my schedule to do the class, but I always knew I would share this clay sculpture project someday.

I thought as a performance idea I could have the chickens do a cluck-cluck chorus. They could cluck to a medley of tunes.

**TIP**

✳ *Prepare the polymer clay by first kneading it in your hands until it is soft and easy to shape. This will make your project smoother and neater.*

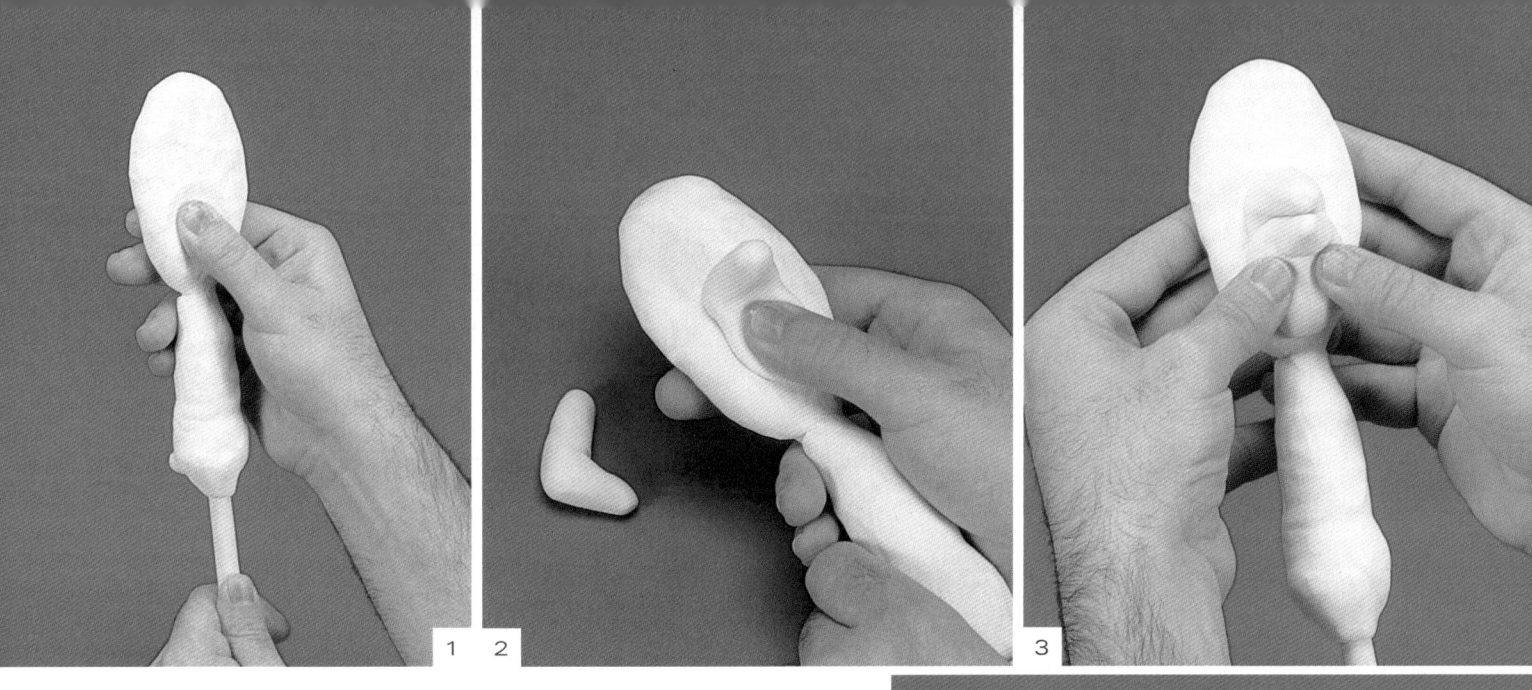

1 Knead the white clay for the body until it is soft. When it is soft, form it around the spoon. The back of the chicken's head will be the rounded part of the spoon, so it is not necessary to cover the entire back of the spoon. Also, add clay around the upper part of the handle of the spoon. This will be the body. Once done, flatten out the mouth area on the head of the spoon, making sure the clay is a little wider than the spoon around the cheeks. 2 Knead the yellow clay for the beaks. Make two L-shaped pieces of clay for the upper and lower beaks. The L-shaped clay, when laid flat, should be a little more than 2" (5cm) long. Place the upper beak in the mouth region of the spoon. Press the yellow clay in and down into the spoon, with your thumb pressing into the bend of the L, flattening the yellow clay on the spoon. 3 Place the lower beak under the upper beak and shape it so the lower beak is wider than the upper beak. Make sure not to press the clay beaks together; they should just rest on each other and fit together evenly. 4 Remove the lower beak carefully from the chicken. With a toothpick, make a horizontal hole in the lower part of the chin section, and another hole through the upper part of the chin section. This will make two holes through the lower beak, for later threading the elastic cord and operating string.

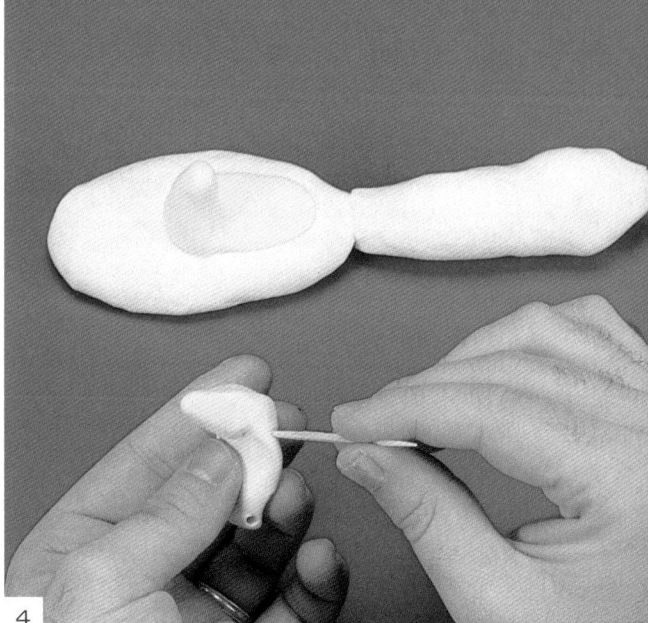

✴ *When making holes in polymer clay, spin the toothpick through the clay rather than just pressing it through. This will make a neater hole and keep the toothpick from messing up your sculptured clay.* TIP

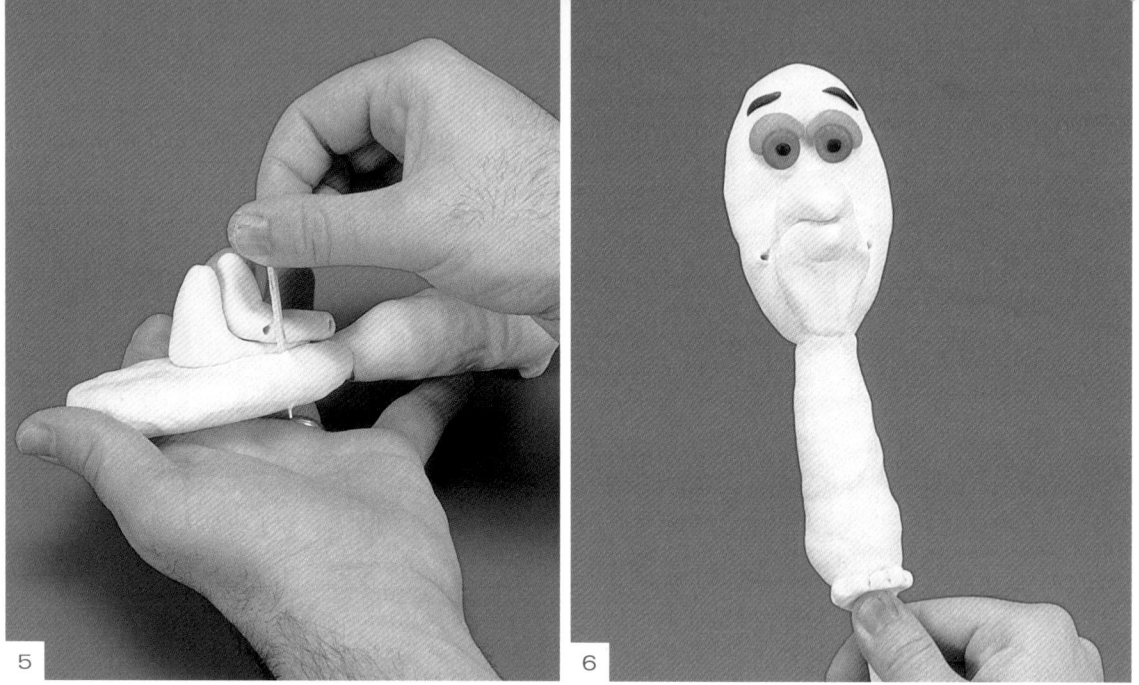

5

6

**5** Place the lower beak back on the chicken. Make two holes in the white clay, through the bunched clay of the chicken's cheeks beside the holes in the beak. **6** Add facial features next. Make jellybean-shaped eyelids with the orange clay. Next, add the blue clay for circle-shaped eyeballs. Add a tiny dot of black clay for the pupils, and just a bit for the eyebrows. Finally, add feet to the Spoon Chicken by making an oval shape in yellow clay and pressing in toes with your fingernails. Push the feet onto the bottom of the body. **7** Smooth the clay body of the Spoon Chicken. Remove any fingerprints or globs of clay. Make sure you don't collapse any of the holes you've made. Then use a toothpick to etch the details of the chicken. Make smile wrinkles in the corners of the mouth and smile lines at the outer corner of the eyes. Add a hole in the center of the pupils, and draw eyelashes on the orange clay. **8** Create the wings by reshaping the white clay of the body. Press the clay between your fingers on both sides of the spoon handle to make wings, then push the clay forward. Smooth the clay again after that.

## TIP

✳ *All polymer clay needs to be conditioned before you use it. Knead each color until the clay is soft, then knead it some more just to be safe. Otherwise, you risk the clay crumbling when you use it, or being brittle after you bake it.*

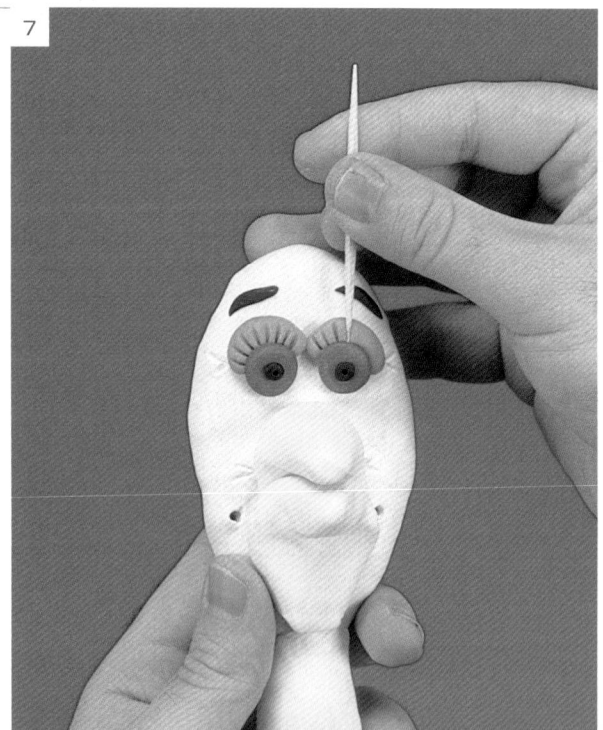

7

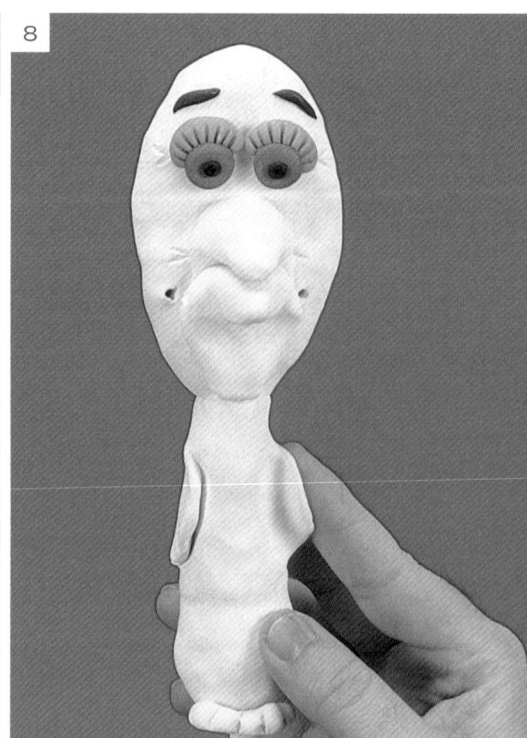

8

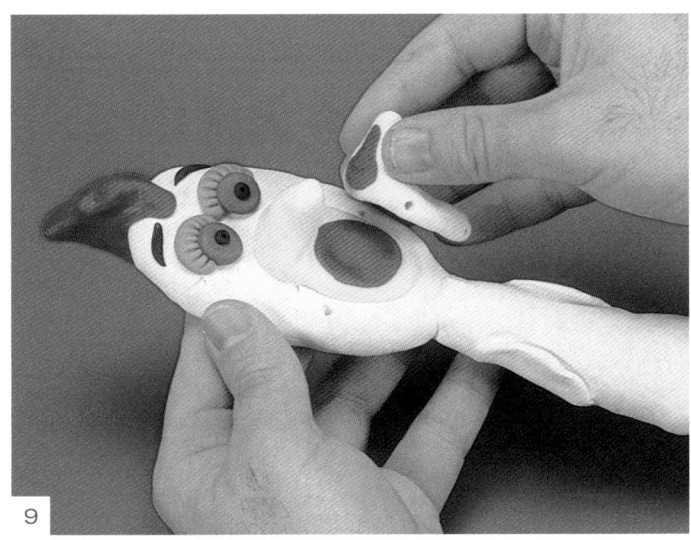

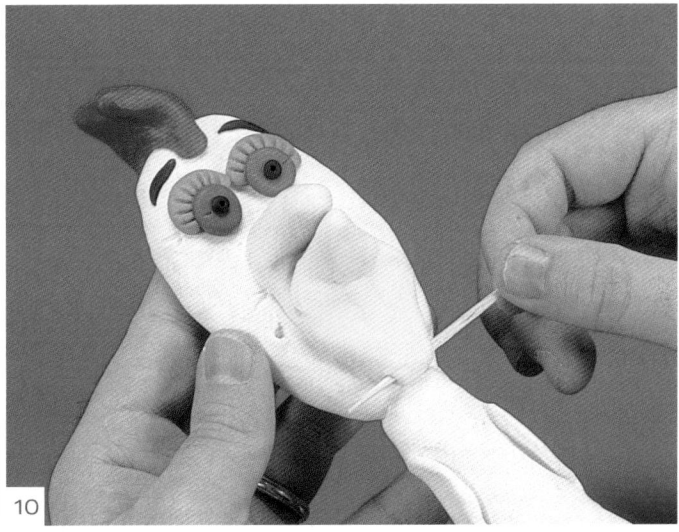

**9** Add the red clay last. Create the comb with a 2" (5cm) roll of clay, then press the clay into thirds, making three lumps. Slowly continue shaping the clay into a flattened E shape. Bend the E shape into a crown and place it on the Spoon Chicken's head. Remove the lower beak and add a flattened red clay triangle for the tongue. Finally, add a flattened pea-size ball of red clay to the throat of the Spoon Chicken. When finished, set the lower beak back in place and make sure it still fits. **10** Prepare to bake your Spoon Chicken. Place the Spoon Chicken on a baking sheet that's covered with aluminum foil. Before you put it in the oven, push the toothpick through all the holes to make sure you haven't accidentally pressed any of the holes closed. After that, bake the polymer clay in the oven, following the directions on the package.

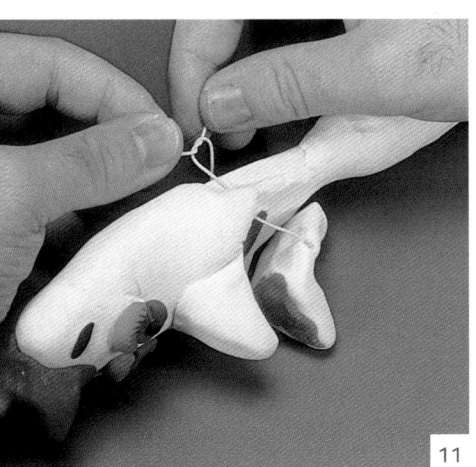

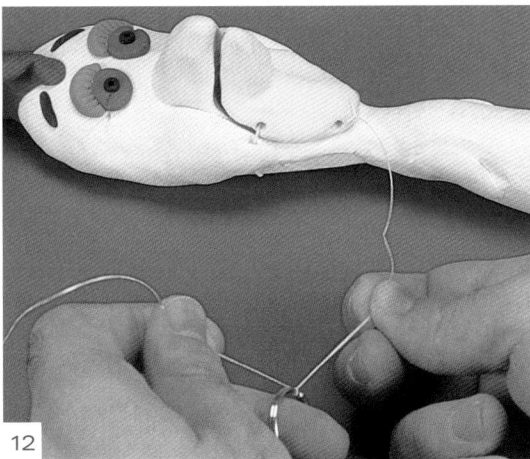

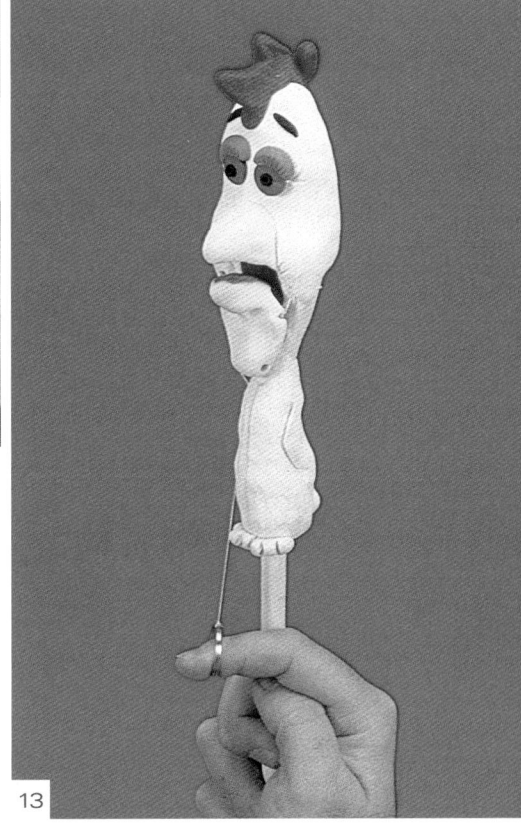

**11** When Spoon Chicken is baked hard and the clay has cooled, thread the elastic cord through the upper hole on the beak and then through the holes in the cheeks and around the back of the spoon. Tie it tight so the mouth is closed. Trim off any excess elastic cord. **12** Thread one end of the string through the lower hole on the beak and tie it off, then tie the ring at the bottom of the string, making sure there is enough string so the ring is below the feet of Spoon Chicken. Trim any excess string. **13** Hold the Spoon Chicken in one hand and operate the mouth with your finger.

**MATERIALS**

13" (33cm) square
of orange short shag fur

3" x 1" (8cm x 3cm) piece
of 1" (3cm) diameter foam rubber

8" x 16" (20cm x 41cm)
piece of yellow long shag fur

two 7" (18cm) diameter paper plates

8" (20cm) square of orange sheet foam

two 16" (41cm) long 5/16" (8mm)
diameter wooden dowel rods

16" (41cm) long 1/2" (13mm) dowel rod

two wooden candle holders with
5/16" (9mm) diameter hole

one wooden candle holder with
1/2" (13mm) diameter hole

27" (69cm) long clothesline

bag of yellow feathers

two 2" (5cm) white pom-poms

two 1/2" (13mm) black pom-poms

black acrylic paint

paintbrush

scissors

glue gun

# DANCIN' CHICK

**puppet** 13 ▶

Another star of my 10-minute puppet show at the Indianapolis Union Station was a stringy-looking puppet named String Bean. I made him dance by attaching his feet to my shoes with dowel rods. His head and arms had rods that I moved with my hands in a criss-cross grip.

With the Dancin' Chick, I use the same grip but the chick has no arms so there's no need to attach its feet to my shoes. Instead I move the head and feet with only my hands. Master this technique and you can perform the Dancin' Chick by yourself. But if you want, you can also hand the feet off to a friend for a more complex dance.

 *If you can't find wooden candleholders, you can use pom-poms or even leave the end of the dowel rods bare.*

**TIP**

1

2

✳ *Make sure you trace your patterns on the back of the shag fur pieces, and cut from the back of the fur as well.*

TiP

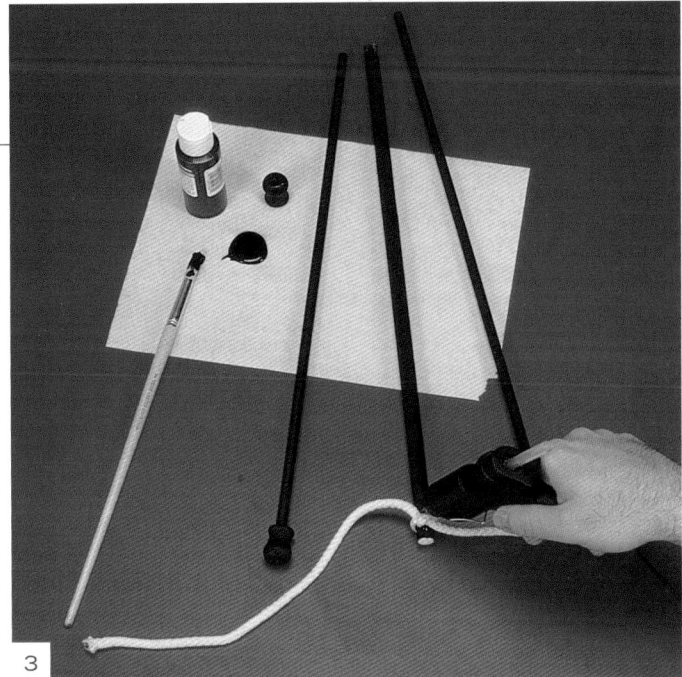

3

4

**1** Using the patterns from page 77 and the orange fur, trace and cut out ten leg cones and the top of the feet. Use the orange sheet foam to trace and cut out the top, bottom and back of the beak, as well as the two feet bottoms. Using a paper plate as a pattern, trace and cut out two body pieces from the yellow fur. Make sure the fur is ½" (13mm) wider than the plate. Cut three 1" (25mm) cubes of foam. **2** Glue one cube of foam to the center of the front side of a plate and one to the heel of each foam foot. Cut slots in both directions in the cubes of foam, using scissors and making sure not to cut the foam in half. **3** Paint the two ⁵⁄₁₆" (8mm) dowel rods, the ½" (13mm) dowel rod and the candle holders with black acrylic paint and let dry. Glue one candle holder on one end of each of the smaller rods. Don't glue on the larger candle holder. Tie the clothesline in half around the ½" (13mm) dowel. The line should be about ½" (13mm) from the end of the rod. Both ends of the clothesline must be the same length. Glue the knot in place on the rod. **4** Glue the yellow shag fur to the back of both plates, including the plate with the foam cube. Center the fur on each plate, and then wrap the fur over the edge of the plate and glue it in place.

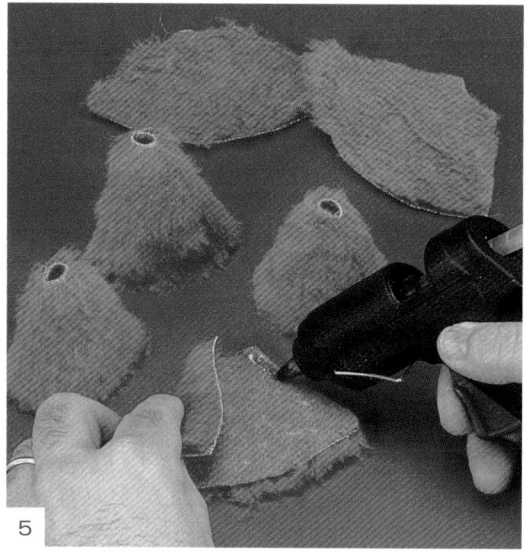

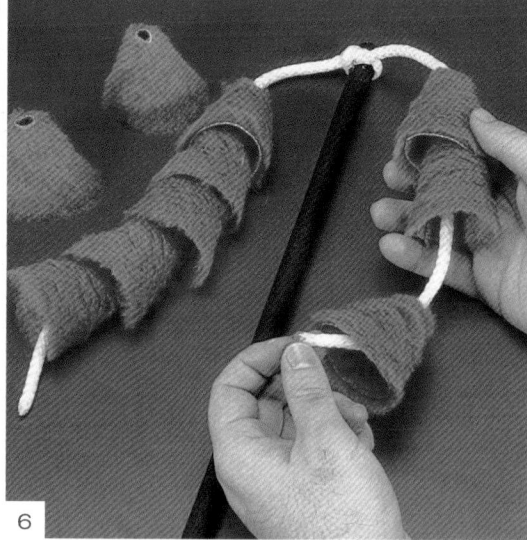

✳ *If you have trouble threading the leg cones on the clothesline, wrap adhesive tape tightly on the ends of the clothesline.*

**5** Glue closed the leg cones. Put a line of glue on an inside edge of a leg cone, and then fold it closed. Do this for all your leg cones.

**6** Thread the leg cones on the clothesline, putting five leg cones on each end of the clothesline.

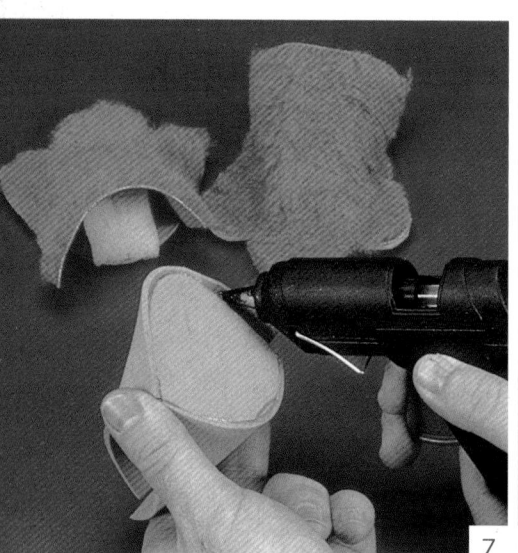

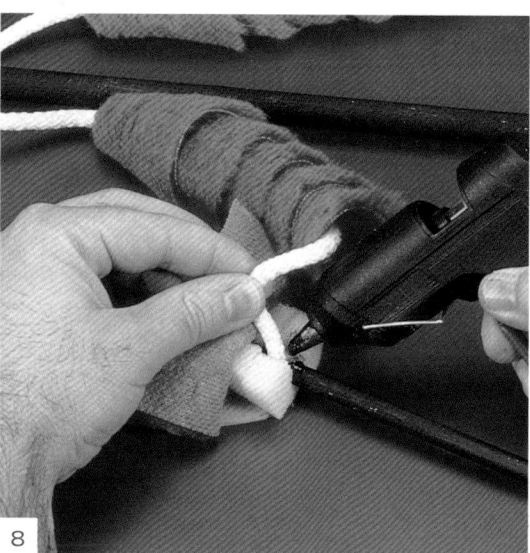

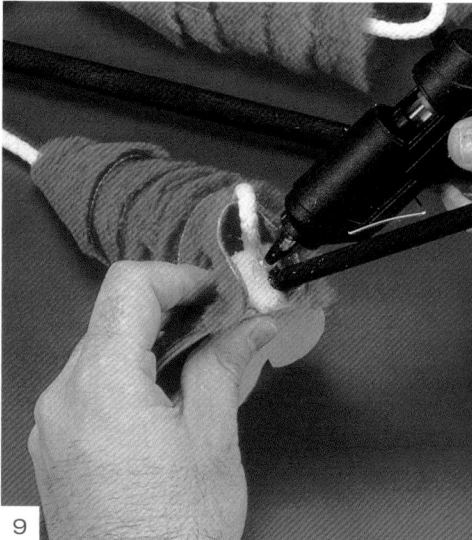

**7** Glue together the top and bottom of the feet, so the orange fur top of the foot goes over the foam cube and the toes match up. Leave the back of the foot open for now. Next, assemble the beak. Glue the edge of the top and bottom beak to the circular back of the beak. **8** Assemble each leg by gluing the end of the clothesline with the leg cones and the empty end of one of the smaller dowel rods into the slit in the foam cube inside one foot. The candle holder will be at the opposite end of the dowel rod. Both the clothesline and dowel rod are attached to the foam cube. Create both legs this way. **9** Close the orange fur on the back of both feet. Seal the end of the clothesline and dowel rod inside the foot. They should be securely attached by glue in the foam cube.

✳ *You have to glue a lot of pieces together in this project. Make sure the glue has secured each piece before moving on to the next step, or your Dancin' Chick may fall apart!*

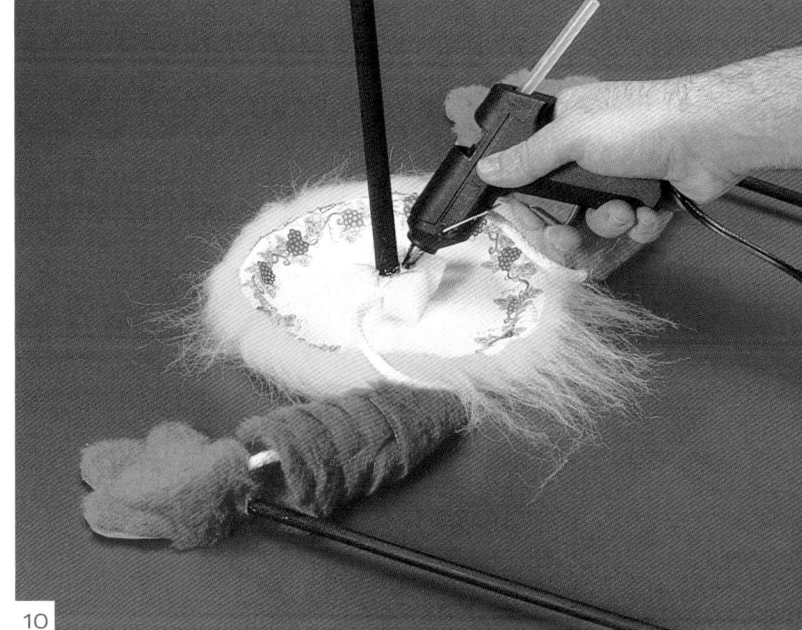

**10** Glue the clothesline end of the larger dowel rod into the foam cube glued on the plate. The clothesline should be glued in the foam cube, as well. Make sure that the dowel rod is in the center of the cube, that the clothesline trails from either side of the foam cube, and that the dowel and clothesline are secure in the foam.

**11** Glue feathers on opposite sides of the plate for the wings. The flow of the fur should be down toward the legs. Keep this in mind as you decide where to place the wings. This Dancin' Chick has five large feathers on each side, but you could also add some to the neck and head of the chick. To glue the feathers in place, add glue to the fur, add the feathers, then secure the feathers in place with more glue.

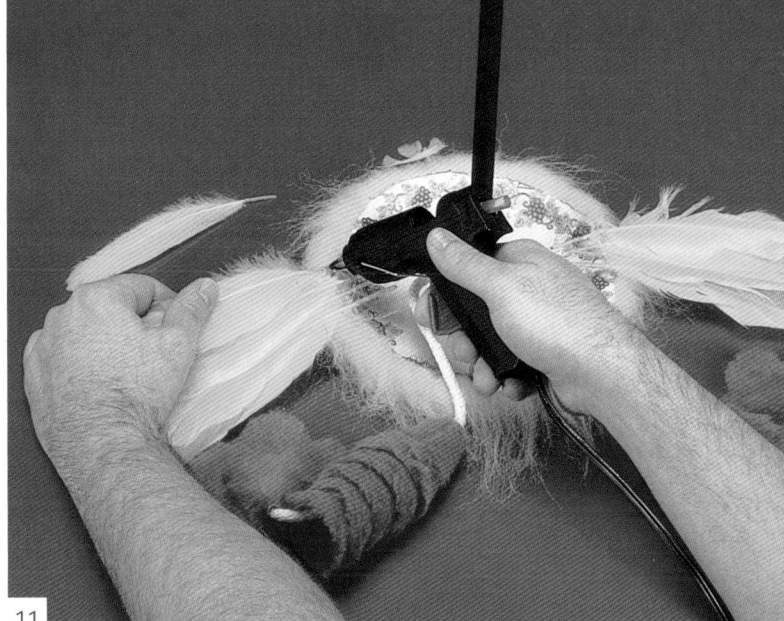

**12** Glue the top leg cone to the edge of the plate. The legs should be positioned on the body of the puppet. Then attach the rest of the cones down the clothesline, each cone evenly spaced and sitting just inside the cone before it. Be careful not to glue the cones together. Put glue on the clothesline where the top of the cone will be, then position the cone on the clothesline.

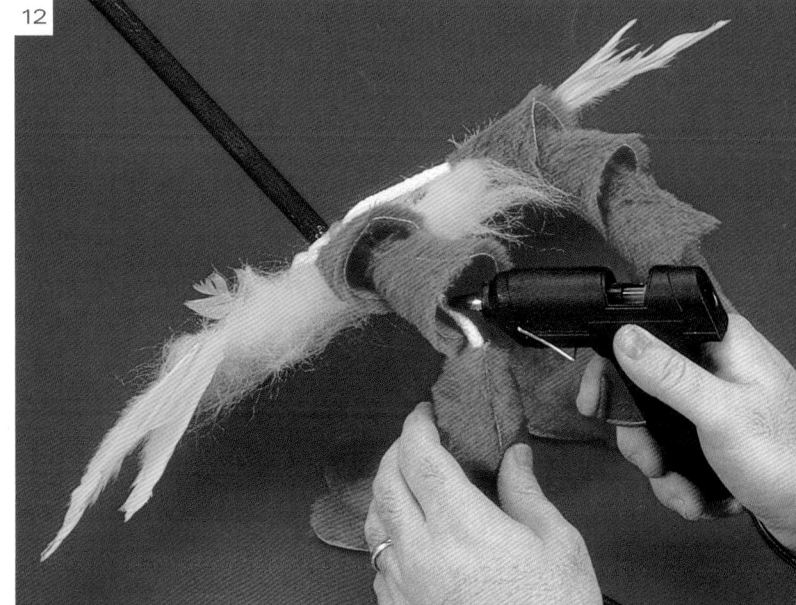

13 14

✳ *Make sure the yellow shag fur on the plate brushes in one direction, down toward the puppet's feet.*

T*i*P

**13** Use scissors to punch a small hole in the center of the back plate of the puppet. Thread the plate down the larger dowel rod and glue the plates together. Glue the candleholder on the opposite end of the dowel rod. **14** Assemble the face by gluing on the beak and eyes. Use the 2" (5cm) white pom-poms for the eyes and the ½" (13mm) black pom-poms for the pupils. **15** To use Dancin' Chick, hold one of the leg rods with your thumb, index finger and middle finger. Hold the body rod with the ring and pinky finger of the same hand. **16** Hold the other leg rod in the other hand with your thumb, index and middle finger. Hold the body rod with the ring and pinky finger of this hand, then squeeze the body rod between the palms of both hands. Your ring and pinky fingers stay locked in your palms while your thumb, index and middle fingers are free to move each leg rod.

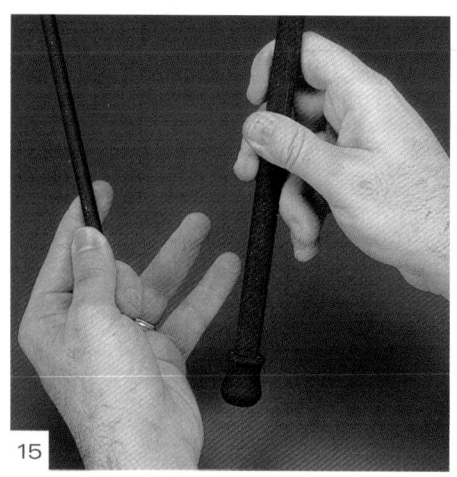

15

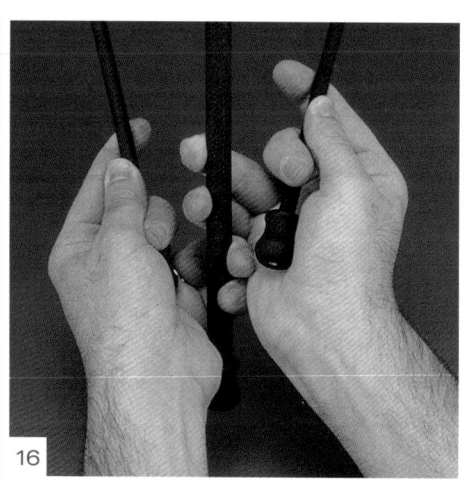

16

☆
## Puppeteering Secret #11

Need some help performing with Dancin' Chick? Turn to page 14 to learn some cool dance steps.

THESE PATTERNS APPEAR AT FULL SIZE.

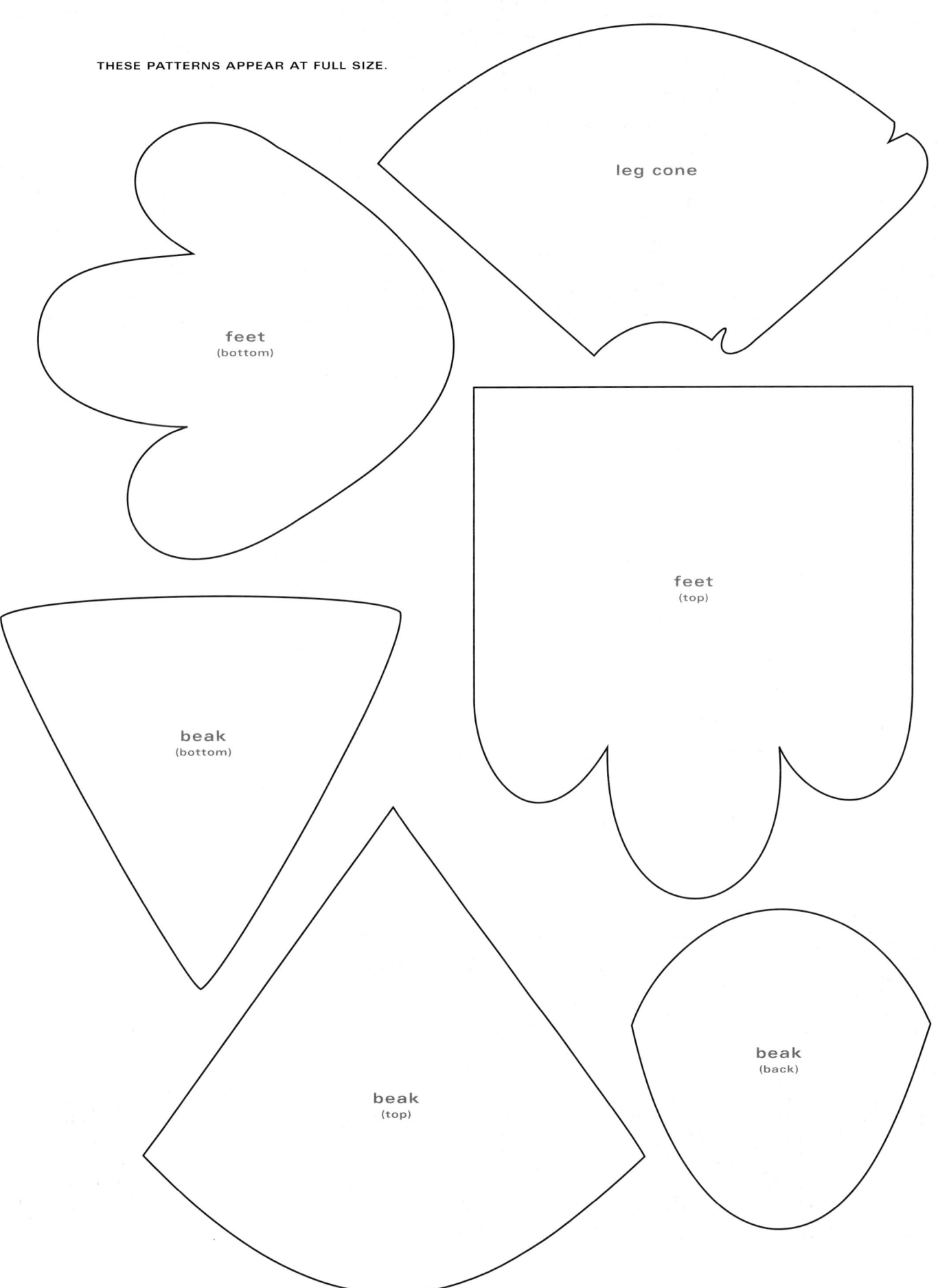

# * Resources

MOST OF THE MATERIALS IN THIS BOOK can be found at your local arts and crafts and fabric stores. For specialty products, here's a list of resources I often use in my puppet building.

## Supplies

**American Art Clay Co., Inc (AMACO)**
4717 W. 16th St.
Indianapolis, IN 46222
1-800-374-1600
fax 1-317-248-9300
www.amaco.com
▸ Polymer clay.

**Aves Studio**
P.O. Box 344
River Falls, WI 54022
1-800-261-2837
fax 1-715-381-2121
www.avesstudio.com
▸ Manufacturer of fine clays and mache's. Web site includes a FAQ page.

**Cottage Industry Miniaturists Trade Association, Inc.**
www.cimta.org
▸ Non-profit organization of handcrafters of dollhouse miniatures. Check the website for a local miniature shop near you.

**FX Warehouse, Inc.**
3500 Aloma Ave. #F17
Winter Park, FL 32792
1-407-679-9621
fax 1-407-679-5609
www.fxwarehouseinc.com
▸ Online ordering and free how-to guides for FX artists and scenic studios.

**The Puppetry Store**
302 W. Latham St.
Phoenix, AZ 85003
1-602-262-2050
fax 1-602-262-2330
Email store@puppeteers.org
▸ Online catalog of the Puppeteers of America.

**Smooth-On, Inc.**
2000 St. John St.
Easton, PA 18042
1-800-762-0744
fax 1-610-252-6200
www.smooth-on.com
▸ Molding and casting supplies.

## Associations

**International Ventriloquists Association**
P.O. Box 17153
Las Vegas, NV 89114
1-702-227-0980
www.inquisita.com

**Puppeteers of America**
P.O. Box 29417
Parma, OH 44129
1-888-568-6235
www.puppeteers.org
▸ National non-profit organization of people who love puppet theater.

# ✳ Index

Animation cel, 22
Antenna, 25
Arm rod, 15, 52
Audience, 7, 10–14, 26, 48, 55
Audition, 56

Baby Kangaroo, 53
Baby Sinclair, 56
Banana Buddy, 38–41
   pattern, 41
Beak, 69–71, 73–74, 76
Body parts
   ankle, 47, 48
   arm, 28, 38, 47, 48, 52, 53, 72. *See also* Arm rod
   cheek, 49, 69–71
   chin, 54, 69
   ears, 27, 47, 49, 54, 57, 59
   eyes, 10, 13, 16, 20, 24, 27, 35, 37, 49, 54, 56–61, 70, 76. *See also* Eye sockets; Eyeballs; Eyebrows; Eyelashes; Eyelids; Irises; Pupils
   face, 19, 20, 25, 39–40, 44, 49–50, 57, 59–60, 66. *See also* Facial details; Facial expressions
   feet, 47, 48, 54, 63–65, 70, 72–74, 76. *See also* Heel; Toes
   finger, 48, 50, 71, 76. See also Thumb
   hair, 66. *See also* Head, fur
   hands, 54, 63–66, 68, 72, 76. *See also* Palms
   head, 32, 36, 37, 49, 54, 57, 60, 65–66, 69, 71–72, 75
   jaw, 19, 20
   legs, 22, 24–25, 28, 35–36, 38, 46–47, 50, 65, 73–76
   mouth, 10, 12–13, 16, 18–20, 24, 27, 31–33, 35, 39–41, 43–45, 57–59, 65–66, 69–71. *See also* Lips; Teeth; Tongue
   neck, 53–54, 75
   nose, 27, 32, 39–40, 49, 54, 60, 66. *See also* Nostrils
   throat, 71
   torso, 47–48
Body movements, 12–13
   blink, 58, 61
   box, 15, 55
   dance, 7, 14, 72, 76
   eye-closing gag, 60
   handshake, 15, 52
   peekaboo, 34
   punch, 15, 52
   sing, 7, 12, 15

   sleep, 13
   speak, 13
   talk, 28
   wink, 13, 61
Body rods, 14
Bottle Bug, 22–25
Bowl of a Thousand Faces, 62–67
   pattern, 67
Boxing Kangaroo, 15, 52–55
   pattern, 55

Candle cup holder, 72–74, 76
Clay, 68–71
Clothes, 33, 50. *See also* Costumes
Clothesline, 72–75
Coaster Creature, 18–21, 42–45
   pattern, 45
Coaster Creature game, 20
Convert-A-Bear, 30–33
   pattern, 33
Costumes, 7, 62
Craft store, 30, 50, 68

Dancin' Chick, 14, 72–77
   pattern, 77
Dastardly Dalmatian, 29
Dinosaurs TV show, 56
Disney World, 56
Drink coaster, 18

Elastic cord, 68–69, 71
Eye sockets, 39–40
Eyeballs, 70
Eyebrows, 39, 41, 70
Eyelashes, 20, 70
Eyelids, 13, 16, 54, 56, 70

Fabric dye techniques, 9
Facial details, 21, 39, 62, 70. *See also* Facial expressions
Facial expressions
   angry, 11
   confused, 11
   envious, 10
   frightened, 11
   hurt, 11
   listening, 13
   love-struck, 10
   proud, 10
   satisfied, 11
   smile, 35, 58, 59, 70
   surprised, 11, 13, 18, 34
Feathers, 72, 75
Foam

   smoothing, 40
   torso, 49
   yellowing, 38
Foamy Farm, 38
Footpads, felt, 48, 51
Fur
   body, 49
   brush, 49
   cut, 46, 49
   fake, 8
   flowing, 47

Glove, 22, 24

Hanger, 52–55
Hats, 50
Head, fur, 58, 59
Heel, 48, 73
Hide and go seek, 60
Hot glue gun, 9, 18, 26

Inspiration, 10
Instruments, 50
Irises, 57

Jewels, 34–35, 37

Kangaroo body, 54
Kids and puppets, 7

Lips, 28, 32
Lip-synch, 12, 15

Masks, 18
Materials, 16, 22, 26, 30, 34, 38, 42, 46, 52, 56, 62, 68, 72
Melodrama, 29
Miss Poodle, 29

Nostrils, 20
Nutty Bear, 13, 16, 56–61
   pattern, 61

Oven, 68, 71

Palms, 48
Paper bag puppet, 16
Performing
   arm rods and, 15
   body rods and, 14
   puppet's personality and, 10
   strolling act, 52
   wearing black for, 48
   *See also* Audition; Puppeteering secrets

Personality, 7, 10, 19, 21, 25, 33
Photo, 42–43, 44
Picture Puppet, 42–45
   pattern, 45
Pupils, eye, 24, 27, 35, 40, 49, 57, 70, 76
Puppet show, 72. *See also* Perform
Puppeteer, 6, 7, 34, 38, 52, 56
Puppeteering secrets
   arm rods, 15
   boxing moves, 55
   dance moves, 14
   emotions, 28
   facial expressions, 10, 13
   lip-synching, 12
   picture puppets, 45
   work gloves, 48

Resources, 78
Running Rabbit, 46–51
   pattern, 51

Santa, 62
Scripts, writing, 7
Sewing techniques, 9, 30. *See also* Stitch, Whipstitch
Shoes, 72
Sock Puppy, 10–12, 26–29, 35
   pattern, 29
Sock Turtle, 34–37
   pattern, 37
Spoon Chicken, 68–71
Spoon, 52–54, 68–70
String Bean, 72
Stitch, running or dash, 9. *See also* Sewing techniques

Tail, 50, 53
Techniques, 9–11
Teddy bear pattern, 30
Teeth, 19, 40, 43, 44, 49
Thumb, 48
Toes, 48, 54, 65, 70, 74
Tongue, 19, 27, 71
Tools, 8
Toothpick, 68–71

Ventriloquists, 30

Walnut, 16, 56, 57
Walt Disney World, 6
Whipstitch, 9
Wings, 23–24, 70, 75